LEGAL ASPECTS OF LAND RIGHTS AND THE USE OF LAND
IN ASIA, AFRICA, AND EUROPE

LEGAL ASPECTS OF LAND RIGHTS AND THE USE OF LAND IN ASIA, AFRICA, AND EUROPE

Ingrid Westendorp (editor)

intersentia
Cambridge – Antwerp – Portland

Intersentia Ltd
Sheraton House | Castle Park
Cambridge | CB3 0AX | United Kingdom
Tel.: +44 1223 370 170 | Fax: +44 1223 370 169
Email: mail@intersentia.co.uk
www.intersentia.com | www.intersentia.co.uk

Distribution for the UK and Ireland:
NBN International
Airport Business Centre, 10 Thornbury Road
Plymouth, PL6 7PP
United Kingdom
Tel: +44 1752 202 301 | Fax: +44 1752 202 331
Email: orders@nbninternational.com

Distribution for Europe and all other countries:
Intersentia Publishing nv
Groenstraat 31
2640 Mortsel
Belgium
Tel.: +32 3 680 15 50 | Fax: +32 3 658 71 21
Email: mail@intersentia.be

Distribution for the USA and Canada:
International Specialized Book Services
920 NE 58th Ave Suite 300
Portland, OR 97213
USA
Tel.: +1 800 944 6190 (toll free) | Fax: +1 503 280 8832
Email: info@isbs.com

Legal aspects of land rights and the use of land in Asia, Africa, and Europe

ISBN 978-1-78068-441-3
D/2016/7849/160
NUR 828

British Library Cataloguing in Publication Data. A catalogue record for this book is available from the British Library.

ACKNOWLEDGEMENTS

This publication is based on the presentations on a land rights conference that was held between 19 and 21 October 2014 in Maastricht. The editor wishes to express her gratitude to the contributors who spent a great deal of time and effort in preparing the presentations and in adapting and updating the contributions for publication.

This conference was the first official starting point of the Land Rights Consortium; a cooperation between the Maastricht Centre for Human Rights and the Maastricht European Institute for Transnational Legal Research (METRO) of Maastricht University on the one hand, and the faculties of law of the Gadjah Mada University (Yogyakarta), Padjadjaran University (Bandung), Udayana University (Denpasar), University of North Sumatra (Medan), and University of Indonesia (Jakarta) on the other hand. Thanks to the financial contributions of the Dutch Ministry of Foreign Affairs, the SWOL, the Research Fund Faculty of Law of Maastricht University, and the Maastricht Centre for Human Rights it was possible to organize this meeting and to invite participants from the Netherlands and abroad, especially from Indonesia.

A word of thanks should also be addressed to Chantal Kuypers and Yleen Simonis, who took care of the organizational and logistical aspects of the conference.

CONTENTS

Acknowledgements v

Introduction
Ingrid WESTENDORP 1

A Human Rights-Based Approach to Food and Land Issues – A Normative Analysis
Fons COOMANS 5

1. Introduction 5
2. The legal basis for food and land as human rights 6
3. Understanding food and land issues: the capabilities and human rights approach 9
4. A framework for analysing food and land issues through a human rights lens 10
5. Security of land tenure through human rights 15
6. A framework law on the right to food 17
   6.1. Introduction 17
   6.2. The aims of a framework law 17
   6.3. The content of a framework law 19
7. Towards a national food strategy 21
8. Extraterritorial human rights obligations 22
9. Concluding remarks 25

Pollution, Takings and Access to Justice in East and West
Michael FAURE and Andri WIBISANA 27

1. Introduction 27
2. Pollution as an externality 29
   2.1. External effects for companies and States 29
   2.2. Internalizing the externality as goal of environmental law 30
   2.3 Possible role of non-legal instruments 31
3. The Coase theorem 32
   3.1 Reciprocal nature of harm 32
   3.2. Conflicting property rights: an example 32

3.3. The Coase theorem: a few constraints 34
3.4. Practical value of the Coase theorem 35
3.5. Nuisance 37
4. First use doctrine 37
4.1. Economic principles 37
4.2. Examples 40
4.2.1. American cases 40
4.2.2. European examples 42
4.3. Economic analysis 44
5. Indonesia 46
5.1. First use in Indonesia 47
5.2. Takings in Indonesia 51
6. Concluding remarks 58

Land Grabbing, Land Struggles and the Human Right to Food
Roman Herre 61

1. A historic starting point 61
1.1. Ongoing social struggles 64
2. Contextualizing land grabbing 65
2.1. ... A convergence of multiple crises 66
2.2. ... Of cases and structures 67
3. Land struggles: the case of Cambodia's 'blood sugar' 68
3.1. The Kampong Speu sugar cane concessions 69
3.2. The role of the European Union 72
3.3. Rightful resistance 73
4. Land struggles: underlying power imbalances 74
5. Contemporary land struggles: complex and multi-layered 75
6. Land grabbing and the human right to adequate food 77
6.1. Access to land and the right to food 78
6.2. Land rights and human rights – a differentiation 78
6.3. Global governance instruments and the issue of democratic legitimacy 80
6.4. A human right to land 83

Women's Right to Land: A Comparison between International Legal Obligations and Customary Laws in Bali (Indonesia) and in Acholi (Uganda)
Ingrid Westendorp and Elin Hilwig 85

1. Introduction 85
2. The international human rights framework relevant to women's land rights 88
3. Indonesia – international and national legal framework 91

3.1. Introduction 91
3.2. International legal framework 92
3.3. National legal framework 93
3.3.1. Constitution 93
3.3.2. Human Rights Act 93
3.3.3. Basic Agrarian Law 94
3.3.4. Marriage Act 94
3.4. Decentralization 95
4. Situation in Bali 95
4.1. Background 95
4.2. Balinese Adat law and tradition on land 96
4.3. Hindu women's land rights; new developments 99
4.4. Remedies 101
5. Uganda – international and national legal framework 102
5.1. Introduction 102
5.2. International legal framework 103
5.3. National legal framework 104
5.3.1. The Constitution 104
5.3.2. The 1998 Land Act 105
5.3.2. National Land Policy 106
5.3.4. Other relevant legal instruments and organs 106
6. Situation in Acholi 108
6.1. Background 108
6.2. Acholi customary law 109
6.3. Acholi women's land rights in practice 111
6.3.1. The current situation 111
6.3.2. Concerns for the future 113
6.4. Remedies 114
7. Analysis and possible solutions 117
7.1. Differences 117
7.2. Similarities 118
7.3. Possible solutions 120
8. Concluding remarks 122

Agrarian Reform and Smallholder Rights in Indonesia: Alternatives to Corporate, Customary and Private Ownership
Ben White 125

1. Indonesian land rights: vision and reality 125
2. Land problems in Indonesia: legacies of the colonial and recent past .. 128
3. Why prioritize smallholder farming? 131
4. Problems of 'customary' and private ownership 133
4.1. Problems of 'customary rights' in land 134

4.2. Problems of private individual titling: the De Soto fallacy....... 135
5. Criteria for alternative land tenure regimes.......................... 137
5.1. The general principle: collective ownership, individual use rights 140
5.2. Using community-owned land to provide use-rights to the poor, near-landless, young farmers, etc......................... 141
5.3. Where private property in land exists, putting a cap on accumulation and speculation 142
5.3.1. Promoting collectively-owned commercial farming, for export and domestic markets........................... 143
5.3.2. Providing and protecting equal land rights for women ... 144
5.3.3. Promoting access to land for young farmers 144

Note on Contributors... 147

INTRODUCTION

Ingrid Westendorp

In October 2014 the Maastricht Centre for Human Rights together with the Maastricht European Transnational Research Institute (METRO) organized a conference on land rights in Europe, Asia, and Africa together with their Indonesian partners of the Gadjah Mada University, Padjadjaran University, Udayana University, University of North Sumatra, and the University of Indonesia. It was the first time that all partners of the so-called Land Rights Consortium were represented at the same conference and this publication is hopefully the first of many that are the product of our cooperation.

Land is regarded as one of the basic needs of a human being and land plays a key role in respect of the realization of a plethora of human rights including the right to an adequate standard of living, food, water, housing, employment, a clean and healthy environment, social status and decision making powers.

Access to and property rights over land are of great concern to all involved in the Land Rights Consortium. In many parts of the world land is scarce and the price of land is high. Land may be threatened by pollution or it may be taken away from small holders because it is needed for large-scale agro businesses or tourist resorts. In many parts of the world, women face discrimination and disadvantage in respect of property rights over land.

The authors of the chapters have put human beings and their needs and interests as regards land at the centre of their respective research.

Fons Coomans makes the link between land and the right to food. The question he raises is how the realization of access to land and food for farmers and consumers can be approached from a human rights perspective. In order to answer this question he takes a normative perspective, analysing relevant hard and soft human rights law. He discusses issues like right-holders, duty bearers, different types of obligations, non-discrimination, protection of vulnerable groups, participation, transparency and the availability of accountability mechanisms and legal remedies. In addition, he touches upon the notion of extraterritorial human rights obligations in the context of existing challenges of economic globalisation and their effects on food.

The starting point of Michael Faure's and Andri Wibisana's chapter is that in the context of pollution a variety of conflicts may arise among various users of land, i.e. holders of property rights over land; either between private parties or between private parties and the Government. They use various examples to show that these types of conflicts may arise both in the East and in the West. Depending on with whom the dispute especially arises, the conflict can be a problem of 'first use' or 'coming to nuisance', or as a 'regulatory taking'. The question they address from a law and economics perspective is how those temporal issues are and should be dealt with, also with a view to an efficient use of the land. While conflicts over land in Europe and the USA are usually dealt with in court, this hardly ever happens in Indonesia. Effective access to justice for victims of environmental pollution or regulatory takings is rather limited and if cases are dealt with in court, they may drag on for years and the outcome may still be very disappointing for the victims. This is illustrated by the *Lapindo mudflow* case.

In his chapter, Roman Herre studies land rights from an NGO perspective. His focus is on peasants, landless farmers, rural youths, rural women, indigenous peoples, pastoralists, fisherfolks and others who need to have access to land for their livelihood. The point he makes is that the social struggle for basic human rights is often ignored in the context of land grabbing. In trying to find solutions to conflicts over land, regulations and guidelines may be drawn up without involving the people who are directly affected. Over the years, multiple global crises have led to land-demanding trends – like the growing of agro fuel – that ignore the need of access to land to grow foodstuffs of small holders and landless farmers. This is illustrated by the 'blood sugar' case in Cambodia and the Barro Blanco hydro dam project in Panama. The chapter concludes with a plea for the operationalization of the human right to land.

Both Ingrid Westendorp and Elin Hilwig discuss the need to examine tradition and customary rules in light of women's right to land in the context of a State's human rights obligations, particularly the obligation to achieve equality between the sexes both in law and in practice. As part of their studies – which they conducted unbeknown to each other – they did field research respectively in Bali (Indonesia) and in Acholi (Uganda). Although the research was done on different continents and there are obvious differences in respect of background and culture, there are far more similarities concerning the influence of traditional customs and laws over women's land rights. In all stages of their lives, women may be dependent on men for access to land and they may encounter additional barriers in respect of property rights over land. It is clear, however, that not all customary laws work to women's detriment; those that are beneficial for women can be maintained, but those that have a negative impact on women's land rights need to be modified.

Ben White's chapter mainly focuses on Indonesia and it raises the question what kinds of land tenure regimes are needed to promote just and equitable access to land for those who need it, and who can make good use of it for the benefit of themselves and society. Smallholder farmers cultivate their land under conditions of insecure tenure in Indonesia which makes them vulnerable to dispossession. Land may be claimed by powerful agribusiness companies and where individual property titles are established there may be a growing situation of inequality of holdings. In many regions the majority of rural households are completely landless, or operate small farms as share tenants on terms that are very disadvantageous. Especially for young farmers it is extremely difficult to get access to arable land. Since the three dominant forms of land tenure - private individual land ownership, customary tenure, and large-scale land concessions - all are problematic, he suggests alternatives that are better suited to present and future challenges and the needs of smallholder farming communities.

Based on the presentations during the conference there was a lively discussion and it became clear that much more research needs to be done into the existing link between land and basic human rights. Particularly the rights of smallholders, male and female, need to be protected in this time of multiple crises and economic globalization where the rights of individuals may be made subordinate to the interests of economic growth of States and large scale agribusinesses. In the framework of the consortium, future research will cover issues as diverse as the influence of tourism on the rights to land and water of local populations, climate change and its impact on the land rights of indigenous populations, conflicts over land between small holders and the palm oil industry, and Muslim women's access to land in case of divorce or widowhood.

A HUMAN RIGHTS-BASED APPROACH TO FOOD AND LAND ISSUES – A NORMATIVE ANALYSIS

Fons Coomans

1. INTRODUCTION

Food issues are prevalent in many societies. The Arab Spring began with popular unrest and riots in Tunisia about rising food prices. In India access to food for the most vulnerable groups in society is a permanent struggle. 800 million people in India have to rely on subsidised rice in order to survive. Farmers in Mozambique have been evicted from their land by companies for the construction of palm oil plantations. Farm land is taken away from small farmers in order to produce biofuels instead. In Europe, a rising number of people pay weekly visits to charity-based food banks to receive food packages to have a few basic meals a week. Many, but not all of these incidents happen as a result of actions of governments and transnational corporations. Economic benefits, making profit, market forces and trade often prevail over the food and land interests of local people and vulnerable members of society. The human rights dimensions of these types of economic processes are often missing or ignored. The purpose of this chapter is to shed light on the normative aspects of food and land issues.

The question that will be discussed is how the realization of access to food and land for farmers and consumers can be approached from a human rights perspective. In other words, what are the components of a human rights approach to food and land issues? In international human rights law a normative framework has been developed which has the potential of guiding the actions of key stakeholders, such as governments, civil society organizations and individuals. The approach which will be followed in this chapter to answer the question identified above is a normative analysis of relevant hard and soft human rights law. The framework that will be applied is a human rights-based approach which consists of a number of principles or components.[1] The different elements of such an approach will be applied to food and land issues. In general, these components include the notions

[1] See generally, http://hrbaportal.org accessed 3 July 2015.

of right-holders, duty bearers, different types of obligations, non-discrimination, protection of vulnerable groups, participation, transparency and the availability of accountability mechanisms and legal remedies.[2]

The chapter will have the following structure. First the legal basis for food and land as human rights will be discussed (section 2), followed by an alternative approach of looking at food and land, namely the capabilities approach (section 3). The next section will discuss in detail what the different components are of an approach of analysing food and land issues through a human rights lens (section 4). Achieving security of land tenure by using human rights will be discussed in section 5. Next, two ways of implanting the right to food will be presented, namely a framework law (section 6), and a national food strategy (section 7). Finally, the notion of extraterritorial human rights obligations will be suggested for dealing with the challenges of economic globalisation and their effects on food and land issues (section 8).

2. THE LEGAL BASIS FOR FOOD AND LAND AS HUMAN RIGHTS

Access to food can be seen as a minimum entitlement to survive. In this regard there is a link with human dignity. The dignity of people who are malnourished or starving is not protected. Human rights are tools to safeguard human dignity. There are various human rights that have links with having access to food on a daily basis. First of all there is the explicit recognition of the right to food in international human rights law.[3] Without being exhaustive, the most important provisions include Article 25 Universal Declaration of Human Rights, and Article 11 International Covenant on Economic, Social and Cultural Rights (ICESCR). The latter provision is quite extensive in laying down different dimensions of food as a human right. First, the right to food is treated as an element of the right to an adequate standard of living, next to clothing and housing. Secondly, access to food not only relates to having enough food to survive, but also to the continuous improvement of living conditions. In addition, the language of Article 11(2) is strong in recognising 'the fundamental right of everyone to be free from hunger'. This treaty provision also elaborates on the need to improve methods of production, conservation and distribution of food and reform agrarian systems. It is clear that food and health issues are very much related. The health condition of a person is subject to the availability and

[2] See for more information, Office of the United Nations High Commissioner for Human Rights, *Principles and Guidelines for a Human Rights Approach to Poverty Reduction Strategies*, HR/PUB/06/12, Geneva, 2006.

[3] For a general discussion see, J. Ziegler, C. Golay, C. Mahon & S.A. Way, *The Fight for the Right to Food – Lessons Learned*, Palgrave Macmillan / The Graduate Institute, Geneva 2011.

accessibility of nutritious food and clean drinking-water. Article 24 Convention on the Rights of the Child recognizes this relationship. More in general, one can say that the enjoyment of other rights depends on having enough to eat on a daily basis to be able to function well as a person. These rights include, for example, the right to adequate housing (relationship between living conditions, prevention of illness and possibilities to prepare meals in a healthy environment). For farmers, the production of food for personal consumption or sale on the market has links with other rights, such as the right to an adequate standard of living (through earning an income), the right to property (property rights over agricultural land), and the right to work (for agricultural workers). Furthermore, plans for agrarian reform require an opportunity for farmers to express their views and participate in the process. It is therefore clear that food as a human right demonstrates the interrelatedness and interdependence of all human rights, economic, social and cultural rights and civil and political rights.

Several proposals have been made to define the right to food. Definitions cannot be found in treaties, but rather in soft law documents. One important example is General Comment no. 12 on the right to food by the UN Committee on Economic, Social and Cultural Rights.[4] In the view of the Committee 'the right to adequate food is realized when every man woman and child alone or in community with others, has physical and economic access to adequate food or means of its procurement'.[5] Another more comprehensive definition is drawn from a report by the UN Special Rapporteur on the right to food, Mr. Jean Ziegler. He suggested that

> 'The right to food is the right to have regular, permanent and unobstructed access, either directly or by means of financial purchase, to quantitatively and qualitatively adequate and sufficient food corresponding to the cultural traditions of the people to which the consumer belongs, and which ensures a physical and mental, individual and collective, fulfilling and dignified life free from anxiety.'[6]

The common elements of the two definitions are accessibility, adequacy and cultural acceptability of food. A related, though separate, notion is food security, which is, however, not a legal concept. Food security 'exists when all people, at all times, have physical and economic access to sufficient, safe and nutritious food to meet their dietary needs and food preferences for an active and healthy life'.[7] This concept is not about rights and right-holders or duties and duty-holders. It should be characterized as a policy objective without an accountability dimension. In general, one can say that access to food can be ensured through three different channels: farmers grow their own food for personal consumption; income

4 CESCR General Comment 12 on the right to adequate food, UN Doc. E/C.12/1999/5.
5 CESCR General Comment 12, para. 6.
6 Preliminary Report on the right to food by J. Ziegler, UN Doc. A/56/210, (2001) para. 22.
7 FAO World Food Summit Declaration, 1996.

generating activities which make it possible to purchase food; social protection schemes and safety nets which either provide for cash transfers to buy food, or food in kind (food parcels).

The legal basis of the right to land is rather different from the one on the right to food. In international human rights law an individual and independent right to have access to land does not exist. The reason for that is that in many countries and societies land is a political sensitive issue which relates to the basic features of how a social and economic order must be organized. For example, whether private property of land must be recognised or whether land is a public good owned by the State. Should land be treated as a commodity which can be traded as a good on the basis of demand and supply, or should the State regulate and control the market for land?[8] As a result there was no agreement among States about access to land as a human right which can be claimed against the State or other actors. Consequently, issues of agrarian reform have also given rise to a lot of debate at the national and international level.[9] One exception to this general omission of land as a human right can be found in the Convention on the Elimination of All Forms of Discrimination Against Women. With a view to eliminating discrimination against women in rural areas, States Parties shall ensure to women the right 'to have access to agricultural credit and loans, marketing facilities, appropriate technology and equal treatment in land and agrarian reform as well as in land resettlement schemes'.[10] It is submitted that other existing human rights, such as food, property, and housing, may be used to define a derived human right to land. This could be defined as the right to own or use land with security of tenure for economic purposes. Creative reading and interpretation of these established rights may result in the recognition of a human right to have access to land. Security of tenure may be seen as a key element and safeguard for being able to use land.

For indigenous groups access to land is of key importance from the perspective of protecting their culture, identity and traditions. The protection of land related rights of indigenous peoples is one of the fundamentals of ILO Convention 169 on Indigenous and Tribal Peoples. The focus of this Convention is not so much on protecting the economic interests of indigenous groups, but rather on the preservation of their cultural identity and traditional values. Articles 13–19 of this Convention on land should be seen from this perspective. In a number of leading

---

8 See G. Meszaros (ed.), *Social Movements, Law and the Politics of Land Reform*, Routledge Cavendish, London 2011.

9 See F. Coomans, 'Agrarian Reform as a Human Rights Issue in the Activities of United Nations Human Rights Bodies and Specialised Agencies' (2006) 24 *Netherlands Quarterly of Human Rights*, pp. 7–31.

10 Article 14(2)(*g*). See on Article 14, I. Westendorp, 'Rural Women's Right to land and housing in Times of Urbanization' in I. Westendorp (ed.), *The Women's Convention Turned 30*, Intersentia, Antwerp 2012, pp. 325–339.

judgments the Inter-American Court of Human Rights has given a dynamic interpretation of indigenous land rights seen from the perspective of the right to protect their communal property (Article 21 American Convention on Human Rights). The Court has said that 'the natural resources found on and within indigenous and tribal people's territories that are protected under Article 21 are those natural resources traditionally used and necessary for the very survival, development and continuation of such people's way of life'.[11] Relevant in this regard is also the UN Declaration on the Rights of Indigenous Peoples which in Articles 26–30 deals quite extensively with different dimensions of land rights of indigenous groups.[12] These include the right to the conservation and protection of the environment and the productive capacity of their lands or territories and resources (Article 29(1)). The key element of indigenous land rights is the link with the cultural identity of the group.

3. UNDERSTANDING FOOD AND LAND ISSUES: THE CAPABILITIES AND HUMAN RIGHTS APPROACH

For many people worldwide being able to have access to food and land is crucial for achieving wellbeing and human development. People have human rights defined as legal entitlements. However, they may lack the opportunities, freedoms or choices in order to be able to live as they would like to do. Amartya Sen and Martha Nussbaum have developed a conceptual approach which has as its main goal achieving quality of life and social justice.[13] The focus of this approach is on the following question: What is each person able to do and to be with a view to achieving human development? In other words, central to this approach are the capabilities of each person defined as substantial freedoms, or opportunities a person has to choose and to act, created by a combination of personal abilities and the political, social and economic environment in which he or she lives.[14] Both Sen and Nussbaum argue that being adequately nourished belongs to basic capabilities (Sen) or central capabilities (Nussbaum). Furthermore, Nussbaum includes in the list of central capabilities control over one's environment which entails being able to hold property (both land and movable goods).[15]

11 *Case of the Saramaka People v. Suriname* [2007] IACtHR 28 December 2007, para. 122.

12 UN General Assembly Resolution A/RES/61/295, 02 October 2007.

13 See A. Sen, *Development as Freedom*, Knopf, New York 1999; A. Sen, 'Human Rights and Capabilities' (2005) 6 *Journal of Human Development* 151; M. Nussbaum, *Creating Capabilities*, The Belknap Press of Harvard University Press 2011.

14 Nussbaum, pp. 17–20.

15 Nussbaum, pp. 33–34.

From a normative perspective there are clear links with right to food and right to land notions. More in general, a human rights approach and human development approach based on capabilities can be seen as complementary.[16] Human rights are defined in terms of rights and duties. These notions can also be used to promote human development in the sense of strengthening the position of people whose capabilities remain unfulfilled by invoking legal language and remedies. In other words, empowerment of people through the use of capabilities can be strengthened by using the language of entitlements. From the perspective of duties, duty-holders can be held accountable for the way human development has been promoted. Furthermore, an important element is the notion of non-discrimination and protection of the vulnerable members of society as human rights concerns which can be useful to make sure that the capabilities of marginalized people are taken seriously by duty-holders. One example is the capability of the Dalits in India to take part in the life of the community and to appear in public with dignity. If we would apply this human development / capabilities approach to food and land issues, then one could argue that a small farmer who has access to land has the opportunity to earn a living and enjoy the right to an adequate standard of living for him/herself and his/her family. On the other hand, if people are deprived from essential foodstuffs, due to man-made or natural disasters, their capability to subsist / survive remains unfilled in the sense that they do not have the freedom to choose a way out. At the same time their right to life / freedom from hunger remains an illusion.

4. A FRAMEWORK FOR ANALYSING FOOD AND LAND ISSUES THROUGH A HUMAN RIGHTS LENS

With a view to giving substance to the right to food and access to land at the domestic level, in this section an analytical framework will be presented. It is based on international human rights law and is composed of a number of distinct, however interrelated elements. It is drawn from different hard and soft law sources and policy approaches drafted and applied within the UN.[17]

When domestic stakeholders and international partners engage in a process of understanding and tackling obstacles to the realization of the right to food and the right to land, the first step should be to identify and assess *the relevant national and international human rights standards and laws.* These include the international treaties to which a country is a State Party, the soft law resolutions adopted by

[16] United Nations Development Program (UNDP), *World Development Report 2000*, Oxford University Press, New York/Oxford 2000, pp. 19–26.

[17] See for example the publication referred to in footnote 2 above.

Member States of the FAO of a normative nature, the relevant resolutions adopted by the UN General Assembly and the Human Rights Council. Secondly, national constitutions are relevant. Constitutions of many States, in one way or another, refer to the right to food, either directly as individual and enforceable rights, or alternatively, indirectly as Directive Principles of State Policy.[18] An example of the former is Article 16 of the Constitution of Bolivia which provides that 'Every person has the right to water and food. The State has the obligation to guarantee food security for all through healthy, adequate and sufficient food'. An example of the latter is Article 16 of the Constitution of Nigeria which provides that 'The State shall direct its policy towards ensuring (...) that suitable and adequate shelter, suitable and adequate food, reasonable national minimum living wage, old age care and pensions, and unemployment, sick benefits and welfare of the disabled are provided for all citizens'. The difference between the two is that in the Bolivian case an individual may invoke his/her rights before the courts and claim that the right to food must be ensured immediately. The Nigerian example entails that the State must take measures to implement the right to food through legislation and other measures with a view to achieving it progressively and within available resources.

Another relevant point in this respect is that international and national standards may contain *freedoms and entitlements* for individuals. This means for example the freedom of peasants or occupiers not to be arbitrarily evicted from plots of land they use. This is a negative obligation for the State. An example is the protection provided in the South African Extension of Security of Tenure Act.[19] An example of an individual concrete entitlement is the Brazilian *Bolsa Familia* scheme which makes monthly allowances for the purchase of food for poor families available.[20] This entitlement entails positive obligations for the State.

The nature of obligations resulting from the right to food or land can be further analysed. This can be done by applying the so-called typology of obligations *to respect, to protect* and *to fulfil*. This typology was developed to clarify the said vague nature of obligations resulting from economic, social and cultural rights. For example Article 2(1) ICESCR refers to the duty to take steps with a view to achieving progressively the rights included in that Covenant. That clause has generally been seen as vague and without specificity. The typology has been developed with the right to food in mind by Norwegian human rights scholar

18 For an overview see FAO, Guide on Legislating for the Right to Food, Book 1, FAO, Rome 2009, pp. 31–49. Also available on-line at www.fao.org and on CD-ROM.

19 Act 62 of 1997.

20 'Brazil's Bolsa Familia scheme marks a decade of pioneering poverty relief', *The Guardian*, 17 December 2013, www.theguardian.com/global-development/2013/dec/17/brazil-bolsa-familia-decade-anniversary-poverty-relief, accessed 9 July 2015.

Asbjørn Eide in the 1980s.[21] The obligation to respect requires the State to abstain from interfering in the free exercise or enjoyment of the right to food by an individual. This is a negative obligation. For example, the State must not evict farmers from agricultural land, nor should it reduce food subsidies in a sudden and arbitrary manner. The obligation to protect requires the State to prevent non-State actors from abusing the right to food or land of the individual. This is a positive obligation. For example, the State must prevent big landowners from evicting indigenous groups from their land; take food safety measures to protect consumers; regulate food prices. Finally, the obligation to fulfil requires the State to take the necessary measures to ensure the satisfaction of the food or land needs of the individual which cannot be ensured by the personal efforts of that individual. This is a positive obligation. The obligation to fulfil has two dimensions: to facilitate: to promote access to means and resources (employment, training, agricultural credit land/agrarian reform). To provide: direct provision of food for those in desperate need through food aid, food subsidies and cash transfers to buy food.

If we talk about a human right to food and land, it means that *right-holders and duty-bearers* have to be identified carefully. In some cases international and domestic standards refer to specific groups that are entitled to protection and special measures, such as rural women (Art. 14 UN Women's Convention) and children (Art. 24 UN Convention on the Rights of the Child). With respect to land rights, indigenous communities need to be identified as holders of collective rights. The same would apply to pastoralists and herdsmen who often use communal land for their live-stock. As part of programmes for agrarian reform, landless farmers may be identified as right-holders of small plots of land, and women as right-holders as part of programmes for agricultural credits and loans. Also women should be treated equally with men as right-holders in matters of inheritance and property rights over land.

When it comes to duty-bearers, the primary duty-holder under human rights law is of course the State. In addition to times of peace during which international human rights law applies, international humanitarian law applies in situations of international and non-international armed conflicts as a *lex specialis*. For example, starvation of civilians as a method of warfare is prohibited. Parties in an armed conflict are also prohibited from attacking, destroying or removing foodstuffs, agricultural areas, crops, live-stock and drinking water installations.[22]

---

21 A. Eide, Report on the Right to Adequate Food as a Human Right, UN Doc. E/CN.4/Sub.2/1987/23 (1987). For an extensive discussion of the typology of obligations approach, see M. Sepúlveda, *The Nature of the Obligations under the International Covenant on Economic, Social and Cultural Rights*, Intersentia, Antwerp 2003, chapter V.

22 Art. 54 Additional Protocol to the Geneva Conventions of 1949 relating to the protection of victims of international armed conflicts, and Art. 14 Additional Protocol to the Geneva Conventions of 1949 relating to the protection of victims of non-international armed conflicts.

Increasingly it is being recognized that *the private business sector – national and transnational – has responsibilities* in the realization of the right to food. Companies should regulate their activities through codes of conduct and live up to the UN Guiding Principles on Business and Human Rights (Ruggie Principles).[23] For example, companies should not bring unsafe food on the market, and should not evict peasants from their land with a view to creating large palm oil plantations. Also international governmental organizations such as the IMF may be seen as duty-holders when they impose lending conditions on Member States that have a negative impact on the enjoyment of the right to food, such as forcing a State to reduce or abolish subsidies on food aimed at lowering the State's budget deficit as a condition for a loan.

Non-discriminatory treatment and inclusiveness must guide all approaches that States adopt aimed at realizing the right to food. This means that in terms of availability and accessibility of food no one must be discriminated on the basis of, *inter alia*, sex, religion, language and ethnic origin. So for example, ethnic minority groups in isolated areas should not be prevented from growing their own food which is culturally appropriate for them. They should be able to exercise food sovereignty. In addition, vulnerable groups in society must be identified and special measures and safety nets must be created for those people whose food situation is at risk and who may not be able to take care of themselves. These may include children, elderly persons, displaced persons, refugees and disabled people.

Another key element of a human rights framework is *consultation and participation* of individuals and communities in decision-making that bears upon their food and land situation. This is very relevant for farmers who face the risk of being evicted from their land, but also when in the framework of programmes for agrarian reform decisions are taken on conditions for obtaining land and related financial requirements and security of tenure. Another example relates to the need to consult, fully involve and seek informed consent of members of indigenous groups when decisions are to be taken that relate to the use of their traditional lands.[24] A related aspect is the need to have transparent decision-making procedures, so that those that are involved, but also outsiders, are able to scrutinize how decisions are prepared and taken.

With a view to clarifying the normative features of the right to food, it is helpful to distinguish between the *Availability, Accessibility, Acceptability and Adequacy of food.* These notions are now increasingly used to clarify the normative

---

23 UN Doc. A/HRC/17/31 (2011).

24 Compare Art. 6 ILO Convention 169 and Art. 19 UN Declaration on the Rights of Indigenous Peoples.

contents of social, economic and cultural rights. With respect to the right to food, availability refers to the possibilities a person has to feed him- or herself directly from productive land, or by using processing, distribution and market systems for food.[25] Accessibility of food has three different dimensions: non-discriminatory access to food as mentioned above; economic accessibility which implies that food must be affordable; physical accessibility which means that food must be within safe physical reach of people, especially for those who are not mobile, such as vulnerable elderly people, sick people, children and disabled people.[26] Acceptability of food relates to the wish of consumers to eat food that is in line with their personal views about healthy food, such as organic food or GMO-free food. It also refers to preferences of consumers to refuse food that is alien to their culture, such as selling fast food in an indigenous village setting.[27] Finally, adequacy of food means that it must be able to satisfy the dietary needs of individuals and be free from adverse substances. Adequacy of food is a relative concept that also refers to the specific cultural, climatic, ecological and socio-economic conditions under which people live.[28]

A final element is the need to have *accountability mechanisms and legal remedies* available which stakeholders and victims can use to denounce policy decisions and violations of rights. Various accountability mechanisms are possible, such as political accountability of government by parliament, national human rights institutes, Ombudspersons and Land Reform commissions. The use of legal remedies has been crucial to denounce violations of rights before courts. Examples relate to stopping evictions from farmland or forcing the government to make food available for vulnerable groups who would otherwise die from hunger.[29] However, so far there have not been many cases where the right to food has been invoked. Perhaps this has to do with the idea that provision of food is often seen as a person's own responsibility, as a private matter in which the State has no role. In welfare States people in need can rely on social security and social assistance schemes to buy food; there is no need to go to court. However, on land issues, special land courts or commissions may be competent to settle disputes on land reform, claims for financial compensation after expropriation and the demarcation of land and the recognition of traditional land rights. For example, there have been several cases on indigenous (Indian) land rights before the Inter-American Court of Human Rights.

---

25 CESCR General Comment 12, para. 12.
26 CESCR General Comment 12, para. 13.
27 CESCR General Comment 12, para. 11.
28 CESCR General Comment 12, paras. 7–10.
29 See People's Union for Civil Liberties *v.* Union of India & Others, Supreme Court of India, Civil Original Jurisdiction, Writ Petition no. 196 (2001). This was a Public Interest Litigation case. Furthermore, Judge declares State of Guatemala responsible for right to food violations, FIAN press release, 16 July 2013, www.fian.org/news/article/detail/judge-declares-state-of-guatemala-responsible-for-right-to-food-violations.

5. SECURITY OF LAND TENURE THROUGH HUMAN RIGHTS

Security of tenure plays a key role in protecting the right to food and access to land for people who make a living by using land as a productive resource. It is an important safeguard aimed at making progress towards strengthening sustainable food security, economic growth, poverty reduction and social welfare.[30] It is very well possible to apply the different elements of a human rights approach to land and food issues, as discussed in the preceding section, to the notion of security of land tenure. Attention for security of land tenure has grown over the years as a result of threats that arise from large investments in land by companies for the production of, for example biofuels or food crops for export purposes. These processes of large scale land acquisition or land grabbing have been criticized from a human rights perspective, because they often go together with loss of land of peasants and indigenous communities.[31] This may lead to loss of income and food for personal consumption. In many cases these land deals take place without proper consultation and compensation of stakeholders. States have facilitated these land acquisitions by providing multinational agricultural companies with the necessary permits, tax advantages, infrastructural facilities and enforcement action, such as a police force to evict people from their land.

States, international organizations, civil society and human rights NGOs have responded to these developments by agreeing, within the framework of the FAO, on a set of Voluntary Guidelines on the Responsible Governance of Tenure of Land, Fisheries and Forests in the Context of National Food Security.[32] The purpose of this document is to act as a framework for regulating and reviewing the planned activities of States and companies in matters of land acquisition, but also for home States where these companies are based. The text as a whole clearly follows a human rights approach by stating as a key objective:

> 'These Voluntary Guidelines seek to improve governance of tenure of land, fisheries and forests. They seek to do so for the benefit of all, with an emphasis on vulnerable and marginalized people, with the goals of food security and progressive realization of the right to adequate food, poverty eradication, sustainable livelihoods, social stability, housing security, rural development, environmental protection and sustainable social and economic development. All programmes, policies and

30 Report of the UN High Commissioner for Human Rights on human rights and land-related issues, UN Doc. E/2014/86 (2014), para. 67.

31 See Oxfam Report *Land and Power*, Oxfam Briefing Paper 151, September 2011, www.oxfam.org/grow, accessed 14 July 2015. See also C. Golay & I. Biglino, 'Human Rights Responses to Land Grabbing: a right to food perspective' (2013) 34 *Third World Quarterly*, pp. 1630–1650.

32 Voluntary Guidelines on the Responsible Governance of Tenure of Land, Fisheries and Forests in the Context of National Food Security, adopted by FAO's Committee on World Food Security on 11 May 2012, www.fao.org/cfs, accessed 14 July 2015.

> technical assistance to improve governance of tenure through the implementation of these Guidelines should be consistent with States' existing obligations under international law, including the Universal Declaration of Human Rights and other international human rights instruments.'[33]

The Guiding Principles of this document are directed to States, but also to non-State actors such as business enterprises.[34] States should, *inter alia*,

- Recognize and respect all legitimate tenure right holders and their rights; to refrain from infringement of tenure rights of others; to meet the duties associated with tenure rights.
- Safeguard legitimate tenure rights against threats and infringements, such as forced evictions.
- Promote and facilitate the enjoyment of legitimate tenure rights.
- Provide access to justice to deal with infringements of legitimate tenure rights.

The language in which these Principles have been drafted clearly links up to the different types of obligations (respect, protect, fulfil) that is well-known in the human rights discourse as discussed earlier. Business enterprises have a responsibility to respect human rights and legitimate tenure rights. This clause is similar to the text of the Ruggie Principles on Business and Human Rights. The Voluntary Guidelines have a large section on transactions in tenure rights as a result of investments in land. In that section it is stated that 'responsible investments should do no harm, safeguard against dispossession of legitimate tenure right holders and environmental damage, and should respect human rights'.[35] The idea that States have an obligation to protect against abuses of rights by business is included in the following way: 'States should provide safeguards to protect legitimate tenure rights, human rights, livelihoods, food security and the environment from risks that could arise from large-scale transactions in tenure rights'.[36]

These Guidelines are an important standard-setting instrument. They describe quite in detail what should be expected from States and non-State actors to protect security of tenure in land matters. Notwithstanding the fact that it is a soft-law instrument, its potential impact may be rather big, because it has been adopted by governments who may also have an interest in complying with the standards agreed upon. In addition, governments may be held accountable for lack of compliance by other stakeholders.

33 Voluntary Guidelines, 1.1.
34 Voluntary Guidelines, 3.1 & 3.2.
35 Voluntary Guidelines, 12.4.
36 Voluntary Guidelines, 12.6.

6. A FRAMEWORK LAW ON THE RIGHT TO FOOD[37]

6.1. INTRODUCTION

As part of the process of strengthening implementation of the right to food, the UN Committee on Economic, Social and Cultural Rights (CESCR) has suggested in its General Comment on the right to adequate food that States Parties to the ICESCR should consider the adoption of a *framework law* as a major instrument in the implementation of a national strategy concerning the right to food. From a general legal perspective, a framework law is meant to cover the whole spectrum of cross-sectoral issues related to a specific subject (such as food security) and to facilitate a more cohesive, coordinated and holistic approach to a specific issue. Such legislation lays down the basic legal principles and competences without a detailed codification. Usually it includes a declaration of objectives and policies, the time frame for achieving objectives, the establishment of relevant institutions and a definition of procedural principles. It may also lay down rules and principles for responsibility and accountability of actors involved and remedies in case of non-compliance.[38] Recently, the FAO has given ample attention to framework laws on the right to food as an important tool to promote the implementation of this human right at the domestic level.[39]

Article 2(1) ICESCR explicitly mentions legislative measures as a suitable means to realize the rights listed in the Covenant. Legislation may be indispensable to comply with the obligation to take steps towards the full realization of rights, as provided for in Article 2(1) and to eliminate discrimination *de iure* and *de facto*. The measures taken should produce results that are consistent with the discharge of a State Party's obligations under the Covenant.[40] Part of such a national strategy could also be to repeal or amend laws incompatible with the right to adequate food, for example, limitations on women's property rights over land.

6.2. THE AIMS OF A FRAMEWORK LAW

The overall aim of a framework law on the right to food is to strengthen and concretize the right to food as a human right in the domestic legal order. We have

[37] This Section is a revised and updated version of parts of F. Coomans & K. Yakpo, 'A Framework Law on the Right to Food – An International and South African Perspective' (2004) 4 *African Human Rights Law Journal* 17, pp. 19–24.

[38] CESCR General Comment 12 para 29.

[39] See FAO, Guide on Legislating for the Right to Food, Book 1, FAO, Rome 2009, Part Three.

[40] CESCR General Comment 9 on the Domestic Application of the Covenant (1998), UN Doc. E/C.12/1998/24 para. 5.

seen above that some countries explicitly recognize the right to adequate food in the constitution, while other countries have a reference to the responsibility of the State for the provision of basic necessities of life, such as food in the constitution. It has been argued by some governments and commentators that a normative expression of the right to food in national legislation is not necessary, because promotion of the right to work and the right to social security are already sufficient to guarantee that people have access to food. In other words, if a person is employed, or failing that, is supported by a social security scheme, the threat of hunger should not arise. It has also been argued that recognizing the right to food at the domestic level as a normative legal expression would bring to light the often stark contrast between government rhetoric and social reality, which is a potential danger for governments. It could lead to social unrest and food riots when the masses of poor people face hunger and malnutrition. Seen from this perspective, governments do not feel a need to incorporate the right to food as a legal norm in the domestic legal order. This kind of reasoning misjudges that providing for the right to food in the national legal order could serve the purpose of establishing and accentuating relationships between rights, such as the right to life, the right to water, the right to health, to work, land, social security and the right to food. It could show that guaranteeing access to food is a complex matter, underscoring the need for an integrated nutritional and health care approach that is mutually supportive. In other words, it would highlight the interdependence of rights and reflect a holistic human rights-based approach to food availability and accessibility issues. Legislation constitutes the foundation for more specific implementation measures. Legislation is required in view of the principle of the legality of administration by governments and is a corner-stone of the rule of law. It is also of particular importance for the recognition and status of economic, social and cultural rights in domestic law.

Another aim of a framework law is to harmonize existing, often fragmented, national regulations, policies and administrative measures on food availability and accessibility from an overall right to food perspective in order to achieve coherence and transparency. A framework law could also serve as a formal safeguard against abrupt and sudden changes in governmental policy, because the law would stipulate the basic principles of the national food policy that can only be amended with the legislature's approval. It should contribute to the entrenchment of the right to food in the domestic legal order and help to strengthen the justiciability of the right to food in individual cases.

6.3. THE CONTENT OF A FRAMEWORK LAW

Prior to drafting a framework law, an accurate and comprehensive analysis of the causes of hunger and malnutrition should be undertaken as part of a national strategy to ensure food availability and accessibility. A national framework law on the right to food would 'translate' the constitutional and/or international provision on the right to food into concrete targets, concepts and definitions, guidelines, powers and policies for implementation in terms of food availability and accessibility. Such a framework law would start by reaffirming the commitment to the right to food as a human right. It would make the right to food operational by identifying target groups, relevant sectoral issues, relevant governmental and non-governmental actors, minimum levels of nutrition and minimum income levels.

The normative content of the right to food should be translated into concrete objectives and related benchmarks to be achieved on the national and local level. Time-frames for achieving targets should be set in the law. In addition, the law should give an overview of the measures to be taken (subsidiary legislation, administrative decisions, income policy, agricultural and agrarian policy, financial grants, tax policy etc.). Crucial is also that the framework law creates a legal basis for the allocation of legal powers to central and local authorities (provinces and municipalities). It is thus important that the law identifies duty-holders at the central and local level. It could provide for coordination of responsibility for implementing the law by assigning responsibility to the different government agencies involved, and give overall responsibility to one particular organ that could perform an overarching function, such as a National Food Authority with strong coordinating, budgetary and technical capacities.[41] A framework law would also include the type and nature of government obligations (to respect, to protect, to fulfil) to give substance to implementation of the right to food. This may also entail identifying the concrete steps to be taken immediately and progressively.

Furthermore, a framework law should take stock of existing sectoral legislation and policy on food-related issues. This may be a very broad spectrum of sectoral areas, such as land reform legislation, land tenure regulations, agricultural policy, access to credit regulations and programmes, access to water regulations, employment policy, housing policy, environmental policy, regulations on food production, food marketing, food quality and food safety, food prices, wage policy, social safety nets and health policy (healthy food). These regulations and policies should be scrutinized from a right to food perspective. Possible conflicts and gaps should be identified with a view to harmonization and filling up. Such a stock-taking exercise should ideally identify the major structural

[41] See FAO, Guide on Legislating for the Right to Food, Book 1, FAO, Rome 2009, pp. 135–147.

obstacles, such as unequal access to land, an uneven income distribution, high food prices, marginalization and vulnerability of specific social groups (landless peasants, agricultural workers, rural women, urban poor) or a lack of training opportunities in the agricultural sector. It could also highlight a lack of adequate implementation of existing legislation.

In order to strengthen the justiciability of the right to food in individual cases, it is important that the framework law provides for a reference to effective recourse procedures in case of alleged violations and indicates which aspects of the right to food are actionable under the law. One may think of court proceedings, administrative review procedures, Ombudspersons or national human rights institutions.[42] Finally, the framework law should include mechanisms for participation of civil society organizations in policy and planning on food-related issues.[43]

Since the year 2000, a number of States have started adopting framework laws on food security. Most of these States are from the Global South. These countries include Argentina, Brazil, Guatemala, Ecuador, Malawi and Uganda.[44] For example, the Law on Food and Nutritional Security of Ecuador of 2006 establishes as a policy of the State 'the food and nutritional security understood as a human right that guarantees the stability of supply, physical and economic access of every person to a healthy, sufficient, safe and nutritious food adequate in quality and in accordance to the culture, customs and preferences of the population, for a healthy and active life' (Article 1). In Indonesia the existing Food Law was revised and now contains stronger elements of the right to food and food sovereignty.[45] One rare example of a State from the North where the idea of a framework law on the right to food has been taken up is Belgium. In January 2014, two Members of Parliament introduced a Bill for a Framework Law establishing the obligation for Belgium to effectively implement the right to food.[46] The overall aim of this Law would be to develop a comprehensive and holistic national food strategy for Belgium's domestic and foreign policy.[47] It seems logical that also Western States develop a coherent food policy to tackle present-day problems, such as unsafe food, unhealthy food, overconsumption and food spoilage, but also food dumping and unsustainable forms of food production. A framework law can provide the legal tools to do so.

---

42 See FAO, Guide on Legislating for the Right to Food, Book 1, FAO, Rome 2009, pp. 164–173.

43 See FAO, Guide on Legislating for the Right to Food, Book 1, FAO, Rome 2009, pp. 157–163.

44 FAO, Guide on Legislating for the Right to Food, Book 1, FAO, Rome 2009, pp. 67–69.

45 Food Law No. 18 (2012).

46 Bill No. 53 3317/001, 28 January 2014.

47 Explanatory Memorandum, para. 9. See also M. Eggen, 'The Law on the Right to Adequate Food: A Necessary Step Against Food Insecurity and Malnutrition in Belgium', *Right to Food and Nutrition Watch 2014*, pp. 74–76, http://rtfn-watch.org, accessed 21 July 2015.

7. TOWARDS A NATIONAL FOOD STRATEGY

Implementation of the right to food for consumers and promotion of access to land for farmers requires the adoption of a comprehensive national food strategy to ensure food and nutrition security for all.[48] The importance of such an approach can be illustrated by the situation in South Africa where around 12 million South Africans are food insecure, while generally it is seen as a food secure country. The fact that food insecurity is often linked to poverty, low or no income and unemployment underscores the need for a holistic approach. Urban dwellers are faced with problems like these, but also people living in rural areas.[49] The detailed Voluntary Guidelines To Support The Progressive Realization Of The Right To Adequate Food In The Context Of National Food Security, adopted by the FAO Member States in 2004 contain elements for such a comprehensive strategy. This is to be a strategy which applies a human rights-based approach and provides practical guidance to States.[50] Guidelines deal with a variety of issues, such as access to resources and assets (labour, land, water, genetic resources), food safety and consumer protection, safety nets for vulnerable groups and markets. For example, regarding the latter the Guidelines emphasize the importance of promoting the development of small-scale local and regional markets and border trade to reduce poverty and increase food security, particularly in poor rural and urban areas.[51] One concrete example in this regard is the need to recognize the importance of informal food traders in urban areas and urban small-scale food production in kitchen gardens. Another one is promoting school-feeding programmes to make use of food produced by local small-holders. There is also the problem that markets do not always function well and that consequently States may be obliged to intervene by controlling and regulating price levels of basic food stuffs or maintaining reserves of essential food stuffs.

One rather recent trend is the emergence of so-called contract farming: 'agreements between farmers and processing and/or marketing firms for the production and supply of agricultural products under forward agreements, frequently at predetermined prices'.[52] The UN Special Rapporteur on the right to food has indicated that such agreements must be assessed from the perspective

---

48 CESCR General Comment 12, para. 21. See also the report by the UN Special Rapporteur on the right to food, UN Doc. A/68/288 (7 August 2013), paras. 42–46.

49 Ensuring food security for everyone, *Pretoria News*, 06 February 2013, www.iol.co.za/pretoria-news/opinion/ensuring-food-security-for-everyone-1.1465314#.VajFDf4w_cs, accessed 17 July 2015.

50 Voluntary Guidelines to Support the Progressive Realization of the Right to Adequate Food in the Context of National Food Security, FAO, 23 November 2004, www.fao.org/human-right-to-food/en/, accessed 20 July 2015. See in particular Guideline 3 on Strategies.

51 Guideline 4.5.

52 Interim Report by the UN Special Rapporteur on the Right to Food, UN Doc. A/66/262 (2011), para. 5.

of whether they contribute to the realization of the right to food and the right to an adequate standard of living for farmers and consumers. A human rights-based approach must be applied when such agreements are negotiated. For example, such agreements must ensure that the degree of competition among traders is sufficient to prevent farmers from being locked into unequal relationships with a particular trader. The Special Rapporteur would be in favour of governments creating an enabling environment for a wide range of options for sustainable relationships between local producers and consumers of food. Market arrangements must be adapted to this.[53]

Another key element of a national food strategy is the development of a system that permanently monitors which groups in society are vulnerable from a nutritious perspective.[54] Not only with a view to preventing incidents of starvation, but also to assess the nutritional status of those groups in society who run a risk of being under- or malnourished. These include new-born children, elderly, patients of infectious diseases, victims of natural and man-made disasters, women, members of indigenous groups and isolated minorities. The latter three may face malnutrition as a result of discrimination. Today, other people also belong to this risk group, such as families in debt who economize on the purchase of healthy food and often rely on charity food banks for which governments take no responsibility.[55] In rich countries other risks are prevalent such as the consumption of unhealthy food by young people and the risk of *obesitas*. On all these groups disaggregated data are required to assess their situation and take pro-active measures to prevent irreparable harm.

8. EXTRATERRITORIAL HUMAN RIGHTS OBLIGATIONS

Traditionally human rights apply on the territory of States which have ratified human rights treaties. They have a territorial scope of protection. All persons on the territory of a State can invoke these rights against the State with a view to seeking protection. As a result of processes of (economic) globalization States and non-State actors increasingly act beyond national borders. Their acts and omissions may have effects on the enjoyment of human rights of people living in other countries. Take the example of a transnational mining company registered in country A which is operating an open pit gold mine in country B and polluting the water of a river which is used by an indigenous group to irrigate the land on which they grow vegetables. As a result of the water pollution the crops become

53 UN Doc. A/66/262, para. 48.

54 Guidelines 13, 14, 17.

55 G. Riches & T. Silvasti (eds.), *First World Hunger Revisited: Food Charity or the Right to Food?* – Second edition, Palgrave Macmillan, New York 2014.

toxic and indigenous people in country B get sick and their right to health is affected. Another example is a big development project for the construction of a dam in a lake in developing country X for which donor country Y provides the funding. As a result of these construction works local residents in country X have to be evicted from their land. The legal questions to be asked are whether countries A and Y are bound by human rights law for their conduct (failure to regulate and monitor the operations of the company, and failure to conduct a human rights impact assessment before the dam was built) which has had human rights effects beyond their national borders. In addition, can these countries be held responsible? These questions relate to the so-called normative gap and accountability gap which have emerged as a result of processes of globalization. These gaps include the lack of regulation and accountability for the activities of transnational corporations abroad; the absence of human rights accountability for intergovernmental organizations; the poor application of human rights law in investment and trade law, decisions and policies; the poor recognition and implementation of human rights obligations in matters of international assistance and cooperation. Many governments argue that human rights only have a territorial scope and they are not bound by human rights law for the effects of activities in other countries. Scholars, UN human rights experts and human rights NGOs have tried to fill the normative and accountability gap by clarifying the extraterritorial human rights obligations of States in the area of economic, social and cultural rights.[56]

The adoption in September 2011 of the *Maastricht Principles on Extraterritorial Obligations of States in the Area of Economic, Social and Cultural Rights* was the outcome of a long process of scholarly research, discussion and drafting.[57] This document is an international expert opinion aimed at restating human rights law on extraterritorial obligations. According to its Preamble 'drawn from international law, these Principles aim to clarify the content of extraterritorial State obligations to realize economic, social and cultural rights with a view to advancing and giving full effect to the object of the Charter of the United Nations and international human rights'.

The notion of extraterritorial human rights obligations is directly relevant for food and land issues in an era characterized by economic globalization. The Maastricht Principles as a normative framework can be a tool to analyse and understand the

56 See for example M. Langford, W. Vandenhole, M. Scheinin & W. van Genugten (eds.), *Global Justice, State Duties – The Extraterritorial Scope of Economic, Social and Cultural Rights in International Law*, Cambridge University Press, Cambridge 2013; Report by the UN Special Rapporteur on the right to food, UN Doc. A/HRC/C/28/65 (12 January 2015), paras. 38–70.

57 For the text of the Maastricht Principles see www.etoconsortium.org accessed 21 July 2015. The Principles were adopted at a conference which took place 26–28 September 2011 at the Faculty of Law of Maastricht University.

extraterritorial conduct of States from a human rights perspective, but these can also act as guidelines for legislation, policies and actions. The Principles apply the typology of obligations (to respect, to protect, to fulfil) to set standards for the conduct of States. A number of examples can illustrate how the Principles may be applied.

The extraterritorial obligation to respect[58] entails that States must abstain from exporting tomato paste and deep-frozen poultry to, for example Ghana, because importing these goods would ruin the opportunities for local farmers to earn a living as a result of cheaper foreign products brought on the market in Ghana.[59] Another example may illustrate that Member States of intergovernmental organizations also have extraterritorial human rights obligations when they act as members of decision-making bodies. In 2014 Member States of the World Trade Organization tried to reach a new world-wide trade agreement on reducing customs and State subsidies for agricultural products with a view to promoting free trade. This would lead to a rise in prices of essential foodstuffs such as rice and wheat for the poor segments of the population. The government of India vetoed the conclusion of the trade agreement, because it would be contrary to safeguarding domestic food security and breach the obligation of the Government of India to protect the fundamental rights to life and livelihood of its citizens.[60]

The extraterritorial obligation to protect requires a State to regulate the conduct of transnational corporations or investment funds registered or domiciled in its territory.[61] One example is the investment by the Sweden-based Global Solidarity Forest Fund (GSFF) in the forest sector in Mozambique. One big shareholder in GSFF is the largest Dutch pension fund ABP. GSFF, through its Mozambican subsidiary Chikweti Forests, invested in tree plantations in the Niassa Province. As a result of these plantations local small-holders partially lost access to land, water and forests. Sweden, as the home State of GSFF, failed to regulate the activities of the investment fund in Mozambique. The Netherlands authorities did not take steps to persuade ABP to reconsider its participation in GSFF.[62] Another

---

58 Maastricht Principles 19–21.

59 See the report by FIAN *Right to Food of Tomato and Poultry Farmers – Report of an Investigative Mission to Ghana*, FIAN, Heidelberg 2007. For more cases see F. Coomans & R. Künnemann (eds.), *Cases and Concepts on Extraterritorial Obligations in the Area of Economic, Social and Cultural Rights*, Intersentia, Antwerp 2012.

60 Statement by Nirmala Sitharaman In Lok Sabha Regarding India's Stand in the WTO, 5 August 2014, www.commerce.nic.in/MOC/press_release.asp?id=3160, accessed 21 July 2015.

61 Maastricht Principles 23–27.

62 For an extensive report on this case see the report by FIAN, *The Human Rights Impacts of Tree Plantations in Niassa Province*, Mozambique, FIAN, Heidelberg 2012.

example can be drawn from the CESCR's Concluding Observations on the most recent Belgian State report. The Committee said that it was

> 'concerned by reports that the State party's policy for promoting agrofuels, in particular its new Agrofuels Act of 17 July 2013, is likely to encourage large-scale cultivation of these products in third countries where Belgian firms operate and could lead to negative consequences for local farmers (Art. 11)'.[63]

The extraterritorial obligation to fulfil has many dimensions.[64] It ranges from an obligation to create an international enabling environment in matters of, for example, trade, investment and development cooperation, to an obligation to provide international assistance. An example of the latter is the Food Assistance Convention which entered into force in 2013. The main objectives of this Convention are to save lives, reduce hunger, improve food security, and improve the nutritional status of the most vulnerable populations by addressing the food and nutritional needs of the most vulnerable populations through commitments made by the States Parties to provide food assistance that improves access to, and consumption of, adequate, safe and nutritious food.[65] The counterpart of the obligation to provide international assistance is the obligation to seek international assistance if a State is unable to feed its citizens.[66]

9. CONCLUDING REMARKS

Over the years we have witnessed a trend of strengthening the normative status of the right to food as a human right. From a short reference to the right to food in the Universal Declaration of Human Rights to detailed soft-law Guidelines relating to legislation and policies on implementation in texts adopted by Member States of the FAO. This process has been fostered by collaborative work of scholars, UN experts and NGOs and civil society organizations. From these developments it has become clear that access to food and access to land (security of tenure) are often very much related. This applies in particular to small-holders, women, and members of indigenous groups who all claim their human rights to make a living and a have a dignified life. However, the normative status of the right to land as an independent human right is still rather weak (with the exception of land rights of indigenous groups). Although there is definitely more attention for land issues in the current human rights debate, so far States have been unwilling to support the right to land as an individual right for those (especially farmers)

63 CESCR, Concluding Observations on Belgium, UN Doc. E/C.12/BEL/CO/4, para. 22 (23 December 2013).
64 Maastricht Principles 28–35.
65 Art. 1 Food Assistance Convention, www.foodassistanceconvention.org, accessed 21 July 2015.
66 Maastricht Principle 34.

whose livelihood depend on the cultivation of land. This is due to the ideological and political dimensions of land and land reform.

The human rights-based approach to food and land issues and its components as explained in the present chapter is a useful normative tool for analyzing and understanding domestic and international developments on land and food issues, such as the practice of land grabbing. This approach can also be used to assess whether legislators and policy-makers at the domestic and international level apply the different components when they take measures to implement the right to food and access to land. If they fail to do so, NGOs and civil society organizations may hold them accountable. Processes of economic globalization add an extra dimension by broadening the spectrum of actors involved, but also by creating normative and accountability gaps in matters of food production, trade relations, investments in food, and land and market forces. The notion of extraterritorial human rights obligations has the potential of laying down standards for dealing with these social challenges. It is up to governments to accept these extraterritorial duties and live up to their human rights obligations which they have accepted voluntarily.

POLLUTION, TAKINGS AND ACCESS TO JUSTICE IN EAST AND WEST

Michael Faure and Andri Wibisana

1. INTRODUCTION

An important question of land rights relates to traditional conflicts which could arise as a result of conflicting uses of land rights. Those types of simple conflicts can arise both in the East and in the West. In some cases, it relates to simple cases of nuisance whereby one neighbour would for instance create a fire in his garden as a result of which the neighbour experiences a nuisance. These types of relatively simple conflicting uses of property rights have always arisen and have in the legal system often been addressed via nuisance law. These types of conflicts between neighbouring properties (and thus neighbouring land rights) have, since industrialization, become slightly more complex and have appeared in different forms. One form is that as a result of economic development more land was needed e.g. for industrial development of land, resulting in particular cases in so-called 'takings'. Those takings have, from an economic perspective, often been justified by the fact that the collective (public) interest would have to receive priority over individual interest. The typical example is a farmer who has to give up his farm land because a school has to be constructed. Human rights have accompanied this process, for example by guaranteeing that no takings without appropriate compensation will take place. Moreover, in recent times more debate has taken place on the necessity of the infrastructural works themselves and in some cases either land owners or NGOs have successfully used their access to justice to fight particular development plans; in some cases arguing that they would not be in the public interest. A complicating factor, especially in developing countries, is that those development projects are often not only in the public interest, but also in the private interest of particular developers. Close connections between the developers and particular politicians may, moreover, seduce bureaucrats or politicians to takings, also in circumstances where it is not obvious that the particular project is in the public interest.

Other types of conflicting uses of property rights have also arisen as a result of polluting activities. Again, the law has – with changing degrees of success –

intervened to award access to justice to victims of pollution and forcing polluters to internalize externalities, i.e. reduce the negative effects of their activities to optimal levels. However, one complicating factor in this respect is the issue of temporal priority. This concerns for example a situation in which a farmer has been farming land that was in his family for many generations. However, circumstances have changed – also as a result of economic development – with the result that houses and residential areas have been built in the vicinity of the farm. In some cases, the situation may arise that citizens living in the residential area will argue that e.g. odours coming from the pigsties of the farmer are causing a nuisance to them, thus requiring the farmer to stop his hindering activities. In those types of circumstances the farmer will often argue that he was the one who first exercised his rights as a result of which potential victims would no longer be able to file a law suit against the farmer. This is, more particularly in common law, referred to as a 'coming to nuisance' defence. It raises interesting questions of conflict that arise between conflicting property rights and the question who, at the end of the day, will have to relocate if, notwithstanding additional efficient preventive measures, pollution cannot be further reduced. The answer to that question not only has a lot of obvious distributional and justice implications, but economic implications as well. Some may indeed argue that if, in our particular example, the farmer were forced to relocate, that this may not provide any incentives to new home owners (and more particularly large land developers) to select locations appropriately. Economists have indeed warned that one should always take into account how particular legal rules may affect the incentives of the stakeholders involved.

In this chapter we want to address these particular types of conflicting property rights, or conflicts in different uses of land rights, not only from a comparative legal perspective (by examining e.g. how these issues are addressed in some European legal systems, in the US, and in Asia, more particularly in Indonesia), but we also want to use an economic perspective; more particularly to examine how different solutions to this issue of conflicting property rights could provide incentives for optimal prevention to the stakeholders involved.

We will first focus on the fact that conflicting uses of property rights whereby pollution is coming from one land affecting another land, can be considered as an externality that has to be internalized (2). Next, we will introduce the *theorem* developed by Ronald Coase showing that – more particularly in rural and indigenous communities where the costs of transactions may be very low – these types of conflicts between property rights will normally automatically be resolved without a need for the legal system to intervene (3). Then, we move to a more detailed discussion of the first use doctrine or, in other words, the coming to nuisance defence. We first sketch how, taking into account the Coase Theorem, conflicts between property rights in situations of temporal priority should be solved. Subsequently, we will provide examples of the US and Europe and apply economic analysis to those examples (4). Then, we move to the situation in Asia and more particularly in Indonesia, showing that not many cases of coming to nuisance are brought to the courts, having largely to do with substantial limits on access to justice for pollution victims. That is the reason why, differently than in the US and in Europe, there is hardly any case law dealing with those issues. Next, we will explain that problems of regulatory takings do often occur, however, also in Indonesia, and that increasingly land owners seek access to justice in order to (in some cases successfully) at least delay or postpone particular development projects (5). Section 6 concludes.

2. POLLUTION AS AN EXTERNALITY

2.1. EXTERNAL EFFECTS FOR COMPANIES AND STATES

The problem of environmental pollution is caused by the fact that some activities which may actually be beneficial, such as the production of pharmaceuticals, can cause negative side effects for third parties, the so-called externalities. These side effects are indeed external to the industrial activity itself since the company committing the pollution is in principle not affected by the negative side effects it causes by its actions. Precisely because pollution is an externality, the starting point of the economic analysis of environmental pollution is that a decision maker, such as the pharmaceutical company of our example, will not take into account the externality when it takes decisions on the production level and the investments in measures to avoid pollution, such as the instalment of a water treatment plant. Environmental pollution is considered by many scholars to be the classic example of an externality.[1]

Not only companies will consider and treat environmental pollution basically as an externality. Also States will in principle do so. Many examples can be given of situations which show that States apparently prefer to export a pollution problem. One example is the granting of licenses to allow for transboundary pollution of rivers; another example can be found by merely looking at the map of Europe and examining the location of nuclear power plants. Apparently most States are inclined to locate nuclear power plants close to their borders causing more dangers for citizens in other countries than for the citizens of the country where the power plant is located. Finally, we can also refer to the global problem of the cutting of the rain forest. This obviously has advantages for the (mostly developing) countries involved that may need the revenues from the sale of timber and cause

[1] See generally R. Van den Bergh, 'Le droit civil face à l'analyse économique du droit' (1988) *Revue Internationale de Droit Economique*, p. 234.

disadvantages mainly to other countries most of which situated in the industrial north. These examples show that not only companies but also States will treat pollution as being external to their own decision making process.

2.2. INTERNALIZING THE EXTERNALITY AS GOAL OF ENVIRONMENTAL LAW

In the absence of the law there will be no incentive for the polluting factory to take the pollution it is causing into account. In other words: in the absence of legal rules the externality will not be internalized. This immediately indicates in a very simple way the goal of environmental law: it should lead to an internalization of the externality by forcing the potential polluter to take account of the pollution it is causing in its decision making process.[2] If the law can achieve this, the pollution would no longer be external to the activity, but would be internalized for instance because the potential polluter decides as a consequence of the pollution to invest in abatement techniques. The body of environmental law subsequently deals with the question how environmental law can give incentives to internalize the externality the pollution is causing. A variety of legal instruments can lead to such an internalization, which will be discussed below.

Also in the interstate context legal instruments will often be used to internalize externalities, meaning that international legal instruments will aim at avoiding behaviour whereby States export their pollution problems. In this respect we can not only point at the whole body of international environmental law[3] but also at the use of national law to fight transboundary pollution.[4] International instruments, especially at the European level, also aim at providing the public at large in neighbouring States with information on potentially hazardous projects in the other States. An example can be found in the (meanwhile often amended) Council Directive 85/337 EEC of 27 June 1985 on the assessment of the effects of certain public and private projects on the environment, also referred to as the Environmental Impact Assessment Directive. Article 7 of this Directive provides that where a Member State is aware that a project is likely to have significant effects on the environment in another Member State, the Member State in whose territory the project is intended to be carried out shall forward the information gathered to the other Member State at the same time as it makes it available to its

2 See M. Faure, 'Economic Aspects of Environmental Liability: An Introduction' (1996) *European Review of Private Law*, pp. 85–109.

3 See e.g. Ph. Sands, *Principles of International Environmental Law, Frameworks, Standards and Implementation*, Manchester University Press, Manchester 2000.

4 See J.M. van Dunné (ed.), *Transboundary Pollution and Liability: The Case of the River Rhine*, Vermande, Lelystad 1991 and J.M. van Dunné, *Non-Point Source River Pollution: The Case of the River Meuse*, Kluwer Law International, London 1996.

own nationals. In addition, this Directive has been amended to bring it into line with the Convention on Environmental Impact Assessment in a Transboundary Context (the so-called ESPOO Convention). According to this amendment[5] there shall be a consultation of the public and authorities in the neighbouring States who can then communicate their opinion on the project to the authorities of the Member State on whose territory the project is located. Practically speaking this would mean that if, e.g., Belgium would decide to locate a new nuclear power plant close to the Dutch and German borders, German and Dutch citizens would be granted a right of consultation and their opinion shall be communicated to the Belgian authorities deciding on the new plant. In addition to this right of information and intervention in the administrative procedure one could, furthermore, obviously also examine whether the location as such could be considered a violation of international environmental law. These examples show that also at the international level legal instruments may particularly be used to counter the possible tendency of States to export their pollution problems.

2.3 POSSIBLE ROLE OF NON-LEGAL INSTRUMENTS

Obviously, one should also mention that legal instruments provide just 'one view of the cathedral' in providing incentives for internalization. One could also hope that such internalization can be achieved through moral persuasion of companies pointing at their responsibility for the environment and for future generations. This might in the end lead to voluntary compliance, although economists are somewhat sceptical about the efficacy of such an approach.[6] Indeed, a company that would invest in expensive abatement techniques for ethical reasons might cause its own downfall since its products will be more expensive than those of its competitors who choose not to install similar abatement techniques. Voluntary compliance strategies may, however, prove to be effective if managers can be given incentives to introduce innovative technologies for preventing or reducing waste streams at the source. Scholars in environmental engineering have powerfully argued that investment in cleaner production technologies will pay for itself.[7] In that sense information strategies can certainly be effective if they can show entrepreneurs that pollution prevention and cost reduction can go hand in hand. However, even if these voluntary compliance strategies are used,

[5] Directive 97/11, *Official Journal*, 7315. For a comment see J.H. Jans, *European Environmental Law*, 2nd ed., European Law Publishing, Groningen 2000, pp. 321–328.

[6] W. Oates and W. Baumol, 'The Instruments for Environmental Pollution' in E. Mills (ed.), *Economic Analysis of Environmental Problems*, Columbia University Press, New York 1975, pp. 95–128. See, however, the work of Menell, who points at the inherent limits of legal institutions in controlling environmental risks (P.S. Menell, 'The Limitations of Legal Institutions for Addressing Environmental Risks' (1991) 5(3) *Journal of Economic Perspectives* 93–113).

[7] See e.g. H.N. Freeman, *Industrial Pollution Prevention Handbook*, McGraw-Hill, New York 1995.

legal instruments may be necessary to give incentives to search for these cleaner production technologies.

The remainder of this chapter will focus on the variety of legal instruments that can be used to internalize the externality. However, a crucial question that comes up in this context is whether there should be an intervention of the legal system to achieve this internalization in the first place.

3. THE COASE THEOREM

3.1 RECIPROCAL NATURE OF HARM

Traditionally, economists advocated the imposition of a tax on polluting activities in order to optimally internalize externalities such as environmental pollution. Since this builds on Pigou's work this tax is usually referred to as a Pigouvian tax.[8] By equalling the marginal tax rate to the marginal costs caused by the harmful activity, the factory from our example would get incentives to reduce pollution in an optimal way. However, in his seminal article 'the problem of social cost' Ronald Coase opposed this idea.[9] Coase stressed the reciprocal nature of harm. In this particular case this refers to the circumstance that the pollution is not just caused by the fact that the factory is emitting harmful substances, but also by the presence of neighbours who are injured e.g. through the smoke emissions. Coase stressed that in these situations there is a conflicting use of property rights. Lawyers traditionally see this situation rather one-sided as one in which the factory limits the rights of the victims by emitting harmful substances. One could, however, equally argue that the victims limit the right of the factory to perform its socially beneficial activities by their presence in the neighbourhood of the factory. One should therefore not automatically ask the question how the law should give incentives to force the factory to reduce emissions. First the question should be asked which of the several actors (factory or victims) should be limited in their property rights. The answer to this question will depend on which of the various actors can take precautions to reduce or prevent the harm.

3.2. CONFLICTING PROPERTY RIGHTS: AN EXAMPLE

This can be illustrated with a simple example. Assume that a factory is emitting smoke, causing a harm of 200 to each of three victims living in its neighbourhood. Assume furthermore that the emissions are only causing harm to the three

[8] A.C. Pigou, *A Study in Public Finance*, MacMillan, London 1951.
[9] R.H. Coase, 'The Problem of Social Cost' (1960) *Journal of Law and Economics*, pp. 1–44.

victims and to no one else.[10] Assume further that there is no feasible way in which the victims could prevent this harm from occurring. The factory on the other hand, could eliminate all the emissions by installing a filter which costs 300. The first question to be answered in this straightforward example is what the optimal result will be: installation of the filter or not. Since a total cost of 600 can be avoided by investing just 300, the optimal solution is obviously that the filter will be installed. The other possible solution would be a relocation of the victims, but we assume that the relocation costs for the three victims would be substantially higher than the 300 a filter would cost.

Graphically the problem could be illustrated as follows:

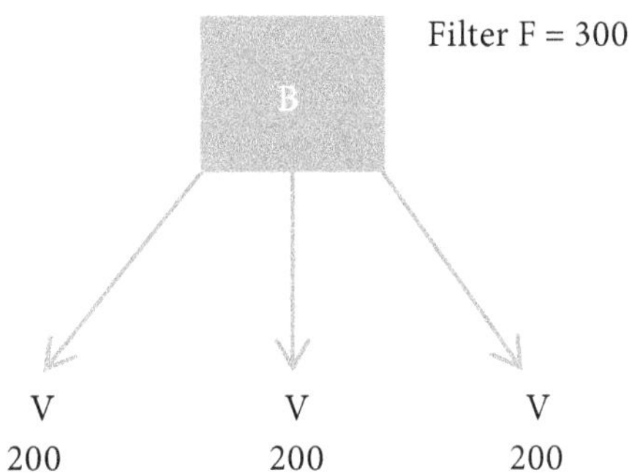

1. Optimum?
   F
2. SL F?
   F+
3. Fault F
   F+
4. No
   F+

This result can be considered quite important, and even as revolutionary since it shows that when bargaining between parties is possible the optimal solution (in this case installation of the filter) will always follow, even if there is no liability. Even stronger: the result will also follow, irrespective of the legal rule, since parties may bargain around in efficient legal rules.[11]

The question then arises whether the optimal solution will follow, being in this case, whether the filter will be installed. Coase holds that if the transaction costs are zero an optimal allocation of resources will always take place, irrespective the contents of the governing legal rule. This is usually known as the Coase theorem. The optimal allocation of resources in this example is obviously the installation of the filter. That is why the optimum (I) is indicated as F (filter) in the box above. Taking up the example we can easily demonstrate that the Coase theorem applies to this case: the filter will indeed be installed irrespective of the contents of the legal rule. If the law holds the factory liable for paying compensation to the victims, the installation of the filter is obviously in the interest of the factory. By installing the

[10] Hence, in this example we disregard the fact that the emissions will obviously also cause harm to the environment as such.

[11] See R. Cooter and T. Ulen, *Law & Economics*, 5th ed., Addison Wesley, Boston 2008, p. 324.

filter which costs just 300 the factory can avoid to have to pay compensation to the victims (of 600). Under this legal regime which could for now be called a 'polluter pays' regime the optimal result will therefore follow. That is why in the box both the strict liability rule (SL) (2) and the fault rule (F) will get an F+, indicating that the filter will be installed. The same is, however, true if the factory is not liable and victims bear their own damage; a 'right to pollute'-regime. Given the zero transaction costs assumption they will get together and negotiate with the factory to convince it to install the filter. By paying the price of the filter to the factory, the victims still are better off since the total costs of the damage are considerably larger than the costs of the filter. That is indicated in the box, where also under no liability (4) the filter will be installed (F+). Hence, in both cases, the polluter pays rule and the 'right to pollute' rule, the efficient outcome will follow.

3.3. THE COASE THEOREM: A FEW CONSTRAINTS

This result, however, merits a few comments.

First it should be stressed that at first sight it is not clear which price the victims will have to pay to the factory for the installation of the filter. Depending upon its bargaining power the factory may well claim more than just the price of the 300 for the installation of the filter. In the end, under a 'right to pollute' rule the victims may have to pay almost up to 599 for the filter if the factory is a tough negotiator.

Second, the efficient outcome will obviously not follow if one of the parties would behave strategically.

Third, the victims must of course have resources available to pay for the filter.

Fourth – and this is a crucial aspect – the Coase theorem only deals with the efficiency effect of social problems, not with distributional aspects. Indeed, although the efficient results will hold in both cases (liability or no liability), there is a distributional difference: in the first case the factory pays for the filter; in the second case the victims pay for it. Hence, the contents of the legal rule will matter from the victims' perspective. This may be the reason why, from a policy perspective, the legislator sometimes intervenes to make the polluter liable even in situations where the conditions of the Coase theorem are fulfilled.

Fifth, the Coase theorem is based on the zero transaction costs assumption. Although many law and economics scholars and environmental economists use the Coase theorem as a starting point for discussing the role of environmental law and, more generally, the need for legal instruments to control environmental pollution,[12] a drawback is obviously that the Coase theorem only works in a zero transaction costs world. In some small cases of pollution it might certainly be useful to apply the Coase theorem. However, in real life situations, the example of one factory emitting smoke that would affect just three victims rarely exists. In most large-scale pollution cases the number of victims will be too large and transaction costs will be prohibitive.[13] Moreover, one aspect of transaction costs is information. It was assumed that the victims and the polluter are fully informed about the damage and about the efficient preventive measures. In many cases that may not be a realistic assumption. In cases where transaction costs are indeed prohibitive the Coasean negotiations will not take place and consequently some kind of intervention of the legal system is needed to effectuate the internalization.

Sixth, so far we have assumed that the various rights are clearly defined and that negotiations take place on the basis of this allocation of rights. Moreover, it was also assumed that the property of the neighbours could be valued objectively. However, in reality subjective valuations, e.g. concerning the importance of the nuisance, could well exist. These may hinder the attainment of an efficient solution through negotiations and can therefore also be considered as transaction costs.

3.4. PRACTICAL VALUE OF THE COASE THEOREM

Critics could argue that the zero-transaction costs hypothesis of Coase's world will never be realized in the environmental context, so that one could question the usefulness of a discussion of the Coase theorem for environmental law. Although many settings in which pollution occurs do indeed involve prohibitive transaction costs, that does not necessarily imply that the Coase theorem would not be useful in this context. The most important implication is that mutually beneficial agreements will be made when no transaction costs prevent parties of making such an agreement.[14]

First, we already stressed that there may be many small-scale pollution cases where factories cause nuisance the effects of which are limited to a restricted

12 B.S. Frey, *Umweltökonomie*, 3rd ed., VandenHoeck en Ruprecht, Göttingen 1992; W.J. Baumol and W.E. Oates, *Economics, Environmental Policy and the Quality of Life*, Prentice Hall, Angelwood Cliffs 1979; W. Oates, 'The Regulation of Externalities: Efficient Behaviour by Sources and Victims' (1983) 38(3) *Public Finance*, pp. 362–375; W. Schulze and R. D'Arge, 'The Coase Proposition, Information Constraints, and Long Run Equilibrium' (1974) 74 *American Economic Review*, pp. 763–772; E.J. Mishan, 'The Post War Literature on Externalities: An Interpretative Essay' (1971) 9 *Journal of Economic Literature*.

13 See on these drawbacks of the importance of the Coase theorem for environmental problems E.J. Mishan, 'Pangloss on Pollution' (1971) 73 *Swedish Journal of Economics*, and W. Kapp, 'Environmental Disruption and Social Costs; A Challenge to Economics' (1970) 23 *Kyklos*.

14 See S. Shavell, *Foundations of the Economic Analysis of Law*, Harvard University Press, Cambridge 2004, p. 84.

neighbourhood. In such a situation Coasean bargaining may be possible. This may potentially be of interest for Indonesia. In some villages there may be small-scale pollution cases where polluters and victims do indeed know each other with the result that bargaining may be possible.

Second, if transaction costs prevent efficient solutions through bargaining, one could examine what the nature of these problems is. If transactions do not occur – for instance because information on the nature of the harm or the potential preventive measures is lacking[15] – regulation could be targeted at increasing the information. If, for example through mandatory disclosure of information transaction costs can be lowered, Coasean bargaining may again be possible. Coase therefore teaches that prohibitive transaction costs should not necessarily lead to regulation determining the standard of safety; the policy maker could also opt for a regulatory solution which facilitates bargaining. Such a solution is obviously less interventionist; it is also more likely that efficient outcomes will occur through these efficient agreements instead of through mandatory regulation.[16]

Third, even starting from the assumption that an intervention of the legal system is unavoidable, the Coase theorem still is useful since it may indicate an efficient solution to the legislator. Indeed: the legislator could ask what solutions parties would have agreed on if Coasean bargaining would have been possible. This presumed result of Coasean bargaining could then be taken as the starting point for the legislative intervention. Thus the legislative solution can 'mimic' the market.

Fourth, an important lesson of the Coase theorem is that parties will, whenever possible (in low transaction costs setting which allow for bargaining) contract around inefficient laws. A nice example concerns some (presumably inefficient) rules of Adat law in Bali containing a prohibition for women to inherit particular family property (real estate). All kind of inventive remedies have been worked out to circumvent these rules, for example the adoption of a boy into the family or the creation of the fiction whereby a girl was considered a boy and thus could inherit. These are examples of remedies to potentially inefficient laws[17] that were created

[15] Asymmetry of information may indeed be one of the reasons why mutually beneficial agreements do not emerge. See S. Shavell, *Foundations of Economic Analysis of Law*, pp. 89–91.

[16] The only question one could ask is to what extent mandatory disclosure regulation is indeed effective in the sense of letting parties make better informed decisions. In the consumer areas there are some doubts whether the disclosure of information (for example forcing people to read before signing a contract) has indeed led to better decision-making. For details see M.G. Faure and H.A. Luth, 'Behavioural Economics in Unfair Contract Terms. Cautions and Considerations' (2011) *Journal of Consumer Policy* 28 June 2011 (online).

[17] In addition to the fact that they constitute clear violations of human rights and of international conventions concerning the rights of women.

in order to allow for an efficient allocation of resources, in this particular case to guarantee that resources could stay within the family.[18]

3.5. NUISANCE

Two doctrines in environmental law are closely related to the situation discussed in the Coase theorem.[19] Both relate to the important point made by Coase that harm has a reciprocal nature. From this follows (1) that it is efficient that both actors take precautionary measures to reduce harm. The law should give incentives for such optimal precautionary measures to both injurer and victims (2) and if there is an incompatible use of property, the efficient solution is obviously not always that the factory should relocate. These issues are addressed in the so-called first use doctrine. It is, however, interesting to point out that this reciprocal nature of harm (stressed by Coase) can also be recognized in nuisance law.[20] The law and economics literature of nuisance law generally holds that both actors should face the social costs of their actions: polluters must pay for incremental harm they cause and victims must not be compensated for excessive harm they could have avoided at a lesser cost.[21] Landes and Posner hold that therefore courts should not award an injunction to stop pollution unless the damage exceeds the costs of abatement.[22] This solution recognizes the reciprocal nature of harm.

4. FIRST USE DOCTRINE

We will now turn to a specific example of conflicting property rights, where various claims collide because of intertemporal differences.

4.1. ECONOMIC PRINCIPLES

The first use doctrine (also referred to as the coming to nuisance defence) relates to discussions that arise when for example a factory was located in a relatively sparsely populated area and is afterwards confronted with neighbours who 'came

18 Some of those rules are discussed in further detail in other chapters in this book.

19 That is why the literature mentions that nuisance cases between neighbours are typically those where bargaining would often occur. See S. Shavell, *Foundations of Economic Analysis of Law*, p. 89.

20 R. Epstein, 'Holdouts, Externalities and the Single Owner: One more Salute to Ronald Coase' (1993) 36 *Journal of Law and Economics*, pp. 553–586.

21 D.N. Dewees, D. Duff and M.J. Trebilcock, *Exploring the Domain of Accident Law: Taking the Facts Seriously*, Oxford University Press, Oxford 1996, p. 267.

22 W. Landes and R. Posner, *The Economic Structure of Tort Law*, Harvard University Press, Cambridge 1987, p. 44.

to the nuisance' and subsequently claimed compensation or even the relocation of the factory. This problem is widely discussed in law and economics literature[23] and more specifically by Wittman.[24]

A starting point in this literature is the question whether the harm to 'newcomers' can be prevented or reduced by preventive measures to be taken by the existing factory. If this is the case and transaction costs are zero then Coase teaches us that the efficient preventive device will be installed irrespective of the legal rule. If transaction costs are prohibitive a liability rule can force the existing firm to implement the preventive measures. If the conditions for liability are met, the existing firm will usually not be successful in claiming the coming to nuisance defence. This is related to the fact that in case law these issues are usually dealt with in an *ex post* perspective, when people have already moved to the neighbourhood of the factory and the question is simply asked in an *ex post* perspective whether or not additional investments in preventive measures could have reduced the harm. Liability law then gives an incentive to invest in efficient safety equipment, even though the victims 'came to the nuisance'. The problem with this solution is that, looking at it from an *ex ante* perspective that it dispels incentives with potential victims not to settle in the neighbourhood of polluting activities.[25] However, it will generally, especially in densely populated areas, be difficult for citizens to choose their residence in such a way that they would never live in the neighbourhood of a factory. The factory on the other hand has the possibility to invest in preventive mechanisms to reduce harm for third parties.

Obviously, many of these conflicting uses of property rights can be prevented if it would be established *ex ante* which area is, given its specific properties, best suited for a certain activity. Wittman argues that the goal of zoning is precisely to determine that e.g. in a beautiful hilly landscape with trees it is better to situate a residential area than heavy industry, taking into account limited transport possibilities, the potential of heavy environmental degradation in this ecologically sensitive area, etc. Ideally, zoning could lead to an *ex ante* fixing of a destination for certain areas.

---

23 See e.g. R. Cooter and T. Ulen, *Law and Economics*, 3rd ed., Glenview, Illinois 2000, pp. 154–159. [NP: pp. 168–174 in the 4th ed.]

24 D. Wittman, 'First Come, First Served: An Economic Analysis of 'Coming to Nuisance'' (1980) *Journal of Legal Studies*, pp. 557–568. See also R. Epstein, 'Nuisance Law: Corrective Justice and its Utalitarian Constraints' (1979) 49 *Journal of Legal Studies*, pp. 72–73; D. Dewees, 'Tort Law and the Deterrence of Environmental Pollution' in T.H. Tietenberg (ed.), *Innovation in Environmental Policy. Economic and Legal Aspects of Recent Developments in Environmental Enforcement and Liability*, Edward Elgar, Cheltenham 1992, p. 143 and T. Merrill, 'Trespass, Nuisance and the Costs of Determining Property Rights' (1985) *Journal of Legal Studies*, pp. 13–48.

25 So D. Wittman, 'First Come, First Served: An Economic Analysis of 'Coming to Nuisance', pp. 567–568.

Problems specifically arise *ex post*, when there are no *ex ante* decisions concerning the destination of a certain area available and in addition a further reduction of harm to the citizens is not possible through cost effective measures. In this respect one can think for example of airports that have taken all efficient noise abatement measures and nevertheless still cause hinder for surrounding neighbours. The question then arises how this conflicting use of the property rights has to be resolved in this *ex post* perspective. In some cases one should examine whether the costs of nuisance have already been taken into account in the price of a certain property, in which case there would already have been a compensation for the externality. Assume that a new railway station is built and that surrounding land is sold for a relatively low price. In such a case the relatively low price a prospective owner pays for the land he purchases can be considered as a compensation for future nuisance to be caused by the railway station. This will then exclude a subsequent claim by the property owner against the railway station. This is not only true for the original owner who purchased at a low price, but also for a subsequent purchaser who would become owner of the piece of land. Again, he should have been informed that the land is close to a railway station (which is obviously easily visible) and he should realize that future nuisance to be caused by the railway station is already compensated for in the relatively low price he pays.

Wittman therefore rightly claims that the foreseeability of the nuisance is an important criterion in most of these cases. A neighbouring owner will have far more possibilities to claim compensation if the harmful activity (which was first relatively innocent) expands in a totally unforeseeable way (for instance because the destination of the area is changed). Once more: if the 'surprised owner' is compensated for the additional harm caused by the unexpected and unforeseeable expansion of the company this compensation is final. This means that he is compensated also for the fact that the price of his land will have decreased as a consequence of the expansion of the particular factory. This entails that a potential new purchaser can purchase the land at a relatively low price, but cannot also claim compensation from the factory since it already paid compensation to the previous owner.

More difficult are situations where the conflicting use of property rights cannot be dealt with by paying compensation for the unreasonable nuisance caused. In some cases the conflict of interest may be so serious that it can only be solved by the relocation of one of the two parties involved. This solution will typically be reached if the magnitude of the damage caused is much larger than the lowest relocation costs. If relocation is therefore the efficient solution, Wittman claims that it will have to be established whose relocation costs are the highest in relation to the importance of the externality caused. If it can e.g. be established that the relocation costs of the existing factory would be much lower than the relocation costs of many neighbours even if they came to the nuisance, the relocation of the factory would still be the efficient solution since its relocation costs are the lowest.

Obviously, the question of who came first will not play a role in answering the question who will have to relocate, but it may play a role when answering the question who will have to pay for the relocation costs. If the new neighbours came to the nuisance in a case of foreseeable harm one could claim that even though the factory will have to relocate (because of the lower relocation costs) the citizens who wrongfully came to the nuisance may be liable to pay (part of) the relocation costs of the factory. The latter is obviously important to give citizens in an *ex ante* perspective correct incentives to choose wisely concerning their decision where to settle. If they settle next to a factory afterwards they can hardly claim that the factory should relocate and should moreover do so at its own costs.

4.2. EXAMPLES

4.2.1. American cases

We can now test these principles of law and economics doctrine by describing how case law deals with this coming to nuisance doctrine. There are two American cases that typically are also discussed in the law and economics literature and therefore deserve to be mentioned here as well. The first is *Boomer v. Atlantic Cement Companies Inc.*[26] Boomer and friends were the plaintiffs acting against a defendant cement company (Atlantic). The discussions in the Court considered more specifically the question what remedy (injunction or relocation) was most appropriate as a reaction to the nuisance caused by Atlantic to Boomer and friends. The majority opinion in the Boomer decision argued that the plaintiffs should be awarded compensation for the infringement on their property rights. The argument against awarding an injunction (which would lead to closure of Atlantic Cement Company) was that Cement Company had invested 45 million dollars in the company and that 300 persons were employed. This refers implicitly to the economic argument that the relocation of the company would probably cost more than the compensation due to the victims. Moreover, the Court held that so-called permanent damages should be awarded, which grants Atlantic Cement Company a permanent right to infringe on the neighbours' property rights, which can also be upheld against future owners of the adjacent properties. In a dissenting opinion Justice Jasen argued against the permanent damages,

[26] *Boomer v. Atlantic Cement Companies Inc*, 26 *NY* 2d 219, 309 *NYS* 2d 312, 257 *NE* 2d 870 (Court of Appeals of New York 1970). Excerpts from this decision have also been published in R. Cooter and T. Ulen, *Law and Economics*, 2000, pp. 155–157 [NP: see pp. 170–172 of the 2004 edition] and in R. Epstein, Ch. Gregory and H. Kalven, *Cases and Materials on Torts*, 4th ed., Little Brown, Boston 1984, pp. 618–624.

arguing that this would be the same as licensing a 'continuing wrong'.[27] Moreover, Jasen argued that paying permanent damages would afterwards remove every incentive of the company to further reduce harm by investing in supplementary preventive measures. However, it appeared from the facts that there were no other supplementary preventive measures available that could have reduced the harm.

Another case that is often quoted is *Spur Industries v. Del E. Webb*.[28] This was a case in the 1950s in Maricopa County in Arizona, about 15 miles west of Phoenix. The farmer Spur had an area suited for cattle and actually kept his cattle on that land. Del Webb, a project developer, buys 20,000 acres agricultural land with the intention to develop a housing area that would be called Sun city. The first houses were built 2.5 miles north of Spur's cattle grounds but in the end 500 houses were constructed and Sun city was expanding. In 1967 Del Webb's project was only 500 feet from Spur's pastures. At that moment Del Webb found out that he was not able to sell the remaining land for residential housing because of the presence of Spur's agricultural activities. Del Webb therefore sued Spur for nuisance caused by smell and flies, Spur having at the time between 20,000 and 30,000 animals on his property.[29] The citizens of Sun city themselves did not file a suit against Spur; only project developer Del Webb. The case was decided by the Arizona Supreme Court. The Court decided that there was a so-called 'public nuisance' because the farming activity by Spur seemed to harm a great number of citizens. In such cases an injunction to stop the harmful activities seemed more appropriate than just compensation, according to the Court. The Court then discussed the 'coming to nuisance doctrine'. Coming to nuisance would have constituted a valid defence if project developer Del Webb would have been the only victim. However, Spur's cattle apparently caused a nuisance to a great number of people (arguing in an *ex post* perspective). Spur on the other hand had not acted wrongfully since he could not have foreseen that in Maricopa County a practically new city would arise in the neighbourhood of his cattle. However, given the interests of the great number of citizens who were victimized the court decided that Spur had to relocate his cattle activities. The Court held: 'Spur is required to move not because of any wrongdoing on the part of Spur, but because of a proper and legitimate regard of the Court for the rights and interests of the public'. However, the project developer Webb is obviously the cause for the duty to relocate that has been put on Spur. Del Webb indeed started activities in an agricultural area whereby it was perfectly foreseeable for him that future house owners could be harmed by the presence of the cattle. Hence, the Court decided that Del Webb had to indemnify Spur for

27 It is the same as saying to the cement company: 'you may continue to do harm to your neighbours as long as you pay a fee for it'.

28 *Spur Industries Inc. v. Del E. Webb Development Company*, 494 p. 2d 701 (Arizona 1972).

29 An interesting detail is that the decision notes that a cow produces on average between 35 and 40 pounds of manure per day, so that 30,000 cows together produce more than 1 million pound of manure per day, which may imaginably cause a smell and attract some flies.

the relocation costs: 'having brought people to the nuisance to the foreseeable detriment of Spur, Webb must indemnify Spur for a reasonable amount of the cost of moving or shutting down'.

4.2.2. European examples

Problems of 'first use' unavoidably also arise in other legal systems. In countries which are traditionally highly populated such as Belgium and The Netherlands there is relatively little discussion on first use. This has a lot to do with the fact that alternative location possibilities are often lacking and it has been decided *ex ante* through zoning and planning laws which kind of activities should take place in a certain area. One can find some cases in which temporal priority seems to play a role. The Dutch Supreme Court had to deal with a case where Van Tol had first use and De Jong knowingly located himself close to the property of Van Tol. When De Jong sued Van Tol because he claimed to be harmed by over blowing seeds, this claim was denied taking into account that Van Tol had first use rights and that the activities took place in an agricultural area.[30] Other examples in which an 'anteriority principle' is accepted in Dutch law are discussed in the literature.[31] Also in Belgian law one can find some rare cases discussing the first use doctrine. If a famous Belgian fries shop chooses its location next to a pig farm, the fries baker should not afterwards complain about the smell emitted from the pig farm.[32] On the other hand, Belgian law apparently also accepts that first use is not a defence against a duty to take additional preventive measures if these can reduce the harm. This duty to reduce the nuisance also exists if the victims came to the nuisance. The Court of Appeals of Ghent held in that respect that the newcomers may expect that the licensee of a factory will take the necessary measures to prevent the harm as much as possible.[33] If additional measures can therefore reduce the problem (of e.g. noise) the first use is no defence against the duty of taking these preventive measures.[34] If, however, additional reduction of harm through further preventive measures is not possible, newcomers cannot claim the closure of the factory.[35] From the facts it appeared that the harm caused

---

30 Hoge Raad (Dutch Supreme Court) 3 May 1991, *Rechtspraak van de Week*, 1991, p. 120.

31 See for instance Court of Appeals for The Hague, 28 December 1988, *BR*, 1989, 769 with case note by P.C.E. van Wijmen; see also the discussion of these cases by R.J.J. van Acht, 'Onrechtmatige hinder' (1993) *Milieu en Recht* 225–226 and by M. Faure, 'Eerstingebruikneming in het milieurecht: een rechtseconomische analyse' in K. Raes and H. Willekens (eds.), *Economische verklaringen van het recht*, VUGA, The Hague 1994, pp. 164–167.

32 Vredegerecht (Justice of the Peace) Beveren, 10 April 1990, *Tijdschrift voor Vrederechters*, 1990, p. 347.

33 Hof van Beroep (Court of Appeals) Ghent, 25 November 1968, *Rechtskundig Weekblad*, 1969–70, p. 429.

34 Rechtbank van Eerste Aanleg (Tribunal of First Instance) Antwerp, 25 June 1981, *Pasicrisie Belge*, 1982, III, 66; Rechtbank van Eerste Aanleg (Tribunal of First Instance) Ghent, 12 March 1981, *Rechtskundig Weekblad*, 1982–83, p. 1327.

35 Antwerp, 17 February 1988, *Rechtskundig Weekblad*, 1988–89, p. 50.

in that particular case was relatively limited, compared to the probably much higher relocation costs of the company, which may have been a decisive factor in the decision.

Issues of temporal priority are also discussed in Norwegian environmental law. The fact that this is apparently a more important issue in Norway (compared to the Netherlands and Belgium) may have to do with the space that is available for alternative locations in Norway, which is largely lacking in Belgium and the Netherlands. Endre Stavang discusses several Norwegian cases which are worth mentioning.[36] Temporal priority is explicitly discussed in cases on airport noise where plaintiffs came to the airport after it was built. In all cases the Norwegian Supreme Court denied compensation. In the first two cases the Supreme Court explicitly denied compensation on the ground that plaintiffs had chosen to come to the airport and thus were nearest to bear the risk of undesirable consequences of this locality choice. In the other two cases the Norwegian Supreme Court explicitly relied on the first use doctrine, arguing that the airport was a first user. Stavang discusses a couple of other cases as well. In one case, referred to as Hunton Bruk, a factory had come to area in 1889, but started to produce a new product in 1957 with new technology. A lawsuit was started by four homeowners who came to the area after the factory had been constructed but before the new technology was installed. The factory argued that it was in the area first and that a new method of production was an expectable development of the activity. The Supreme Court, however, found the factory liable.

Temporal priority apparently plays an important role in French environmental liability law. French law distinguishes between liability based on public law (basically public authority liability) and liability based on private law. In both cases 'first use' plays a role. When a public work has been constructed before the victim 'came to the nuisance' under French law this constitutes a true immunity. Case law apparently holds that in that particular case no compensation is due to the victim or at least compensation can be considerably reduced.[37] The problem is, according to French legal doctrine, that such a temporal priority basically provides the public work a true 'right to pollute'.[38] The only limit to this right is that the public works that have been implanted earlier should not have led to greater nuisance. If the nuisance increased after the original installation, compensation will be awarded. An additional condition for compensation is that this aggravation of the nuisance was not foreseeable for the victim.

---

36 See his unpublished manuscript, E. Stavang, *Tolerance Limits and Temporal Priority in Environmental civil liability*, paper presented at the 13th annual conference of the European Association of Law and Economics, Haifa, Israel. [NP: a version of this paper was published in the (1997) 17 *International Review of Law and Economics*, pp. 553–574].

37 See M. Prieur, *Droit de l'Environnement*, 10th ed., Dalloz, Paris 2011, p. 1074, no. 1277.

38 *Idem*.

Similar rules apply in the context of civil environmental liability. Again, in 1976 the legislator more or less legalized existing nuisances and hence recognized a 'first use doctrine'.[39] It is striking that this 'right to pollute', introduced in French law in 1976, was the result of lobbying by agricultural interest groups.[40] In the words of Prieur, this amendment was the result of the 'bad mood' of a few farmers resulting from abusive law suits filed by neighbours having their secondary residences in agricultural areas and subsequently complaining about noise created as a result of agricultural activities.[41] This immunity has been more or less reconfirmed in a legislative change of 1980, but is heavily criticized in the literature. It is held that as a result of this immunity victims lose their access to justice against polluting activities.[42] Some even hold that this first use doctrine protects polluters and may even constitute a violation of article 8 of the European Convention on Human Rights.[43]

4.3. ECONOMIC ANALYSIS

If one applies the economic criteria advanced by Wittman and others to the cases discussed one could, as far as the American Boomer case is concerned, refer to Cooter and Ulen who argue that the attractive aspect of paying permanent damages is that the conflicting use of property rights is settled once and for all. As a consequence of the payments the externality is finally internalized.[44] Wittman, however, has considerable criticism on the Boomer case. He rightly argues that the first use issue is not at all examined in the case, although it appears from the facts that the home owners were in the area first whereas the harmful activity, in this case the cement factory, came later.[45] Wittman furthermore argues that the economic analysis the Court tries to engage in has many flaws. It does indeed argue that the employment of 300 people and the 45 million dollar investments make the relocation costs for the cement factory higher than for the home owners. This might be true in an *ex post* situation whereby the cement factory came to the residential area. This provides, however, a wrong signal for future companies who

39 M. Prieur, *Droit de l'Environnement*, p. 1081, no. 1286.

40 An Article L421-9 was added to the Code de l'Urbanisme holding 'Damage caused to the occupant of a building by nuisances resulting from agricultural, industrial or commercial activities do not give raise to a right to compensation when the construction permit related to the building that is exposed to the nuisances has been demanded after the existence of the activities that caused the nuisance and when these activities have been continued in the same circumstances'.

41 See M. Prieur, 'Le parlement contre l'environnement' (1977) *Revue Juridique de l'Environnement*, p. 131.

42 M. Prieur, *Droit de l'Environnement*, p. 1083, no. 1288.

43 M. Prieur, *Droit de l'Environnement*, p. 1084.

44 R. Cooter and T. Ulen, *Law & Economics*, 154–157 [NP: in the 2004 edition: see pp. 168–172].

45 D. Wittman, 'First Come, First Served: An Economic Analysis of 'Coming to Nuisance', p. 558.

have to make a similar decision in an *ex ante* perspective. The Boomer decision seems to indicate that once a company has made considerable investments and the employees are there, the relocation is not necessary any longer and a payoff with permanent damages will suffice. Wittman correctly argues that the Court should have examined in an *ex ante* perspective whether the cement factory had a variety of possibilities of location and whether it chose its location in the residential area wisely. It is, moreover, striking, that in the assessment of the necessity to relocate the Court only addresses the high relocation costs for the cement factory and does not even calculate the potential relocation costs for Boomer and the other home owners (who even were there first).[46] Whether the Boomer case was correctly decided from an economic point of view is therefore hard to say since the court did not involve all the relevant costs in deciding the case and did not at all discuss the issue that the home owners were there first and the cement factory caused the nuisance by a potentially wrongful location decision.

This is different in the other American case *Spur v. Del Webb*. In that case the first use issue is discussed by the Court. Looking at the decision from an economic point of view one can say that it was totally unforeseeable for the cattle owner Spur that project developer Del Webb would come to the particular area. Nevertheless, the coming to nuisance defence that Spur invoked is rejected and he is forced to relocate since his relocation costs were lower than the relocation costs of the 500 home owners. This makes sense from an economic point of view. But since the project developer Webb was wrongful in an *ex ante* perspective by taking the decision to locate near to an agricultural area with 30,000 cows, it is equally correct to decide that project developer Del Webb has to compensate Spur. Were this not the case, then this would give totally wrong incentives to future project developers. Hence, in that particular case an efficient solution is reached from an *ex post* perspective since the activity with the lowest relocation costs has to disappear, whereby, moreover the prospective project developers will still have correct incentives *ex ante* by forcing Del Webb to pay for Spur's relocation.[47] This solution is also referred to as a 'purchased injunction': the newcomer can 'purchase' an injunction, meaning that he can claim the closure of the activity that is causing the nuisance if he is prepared to compensate the relocation costs.[48]

Also the Dutch, Belgian and Norwegian cases seem to comply with the economic rules of thumb sketched above. Coming to nuisance is accepted as a defence if

[46] D. Wittman, 'First Come, First Served: An Economic Analysis of 'Coming to Nuisance', p. 563.

[47] So D. Wittman, 'First Come, First Served: An Economic Analysis of 'Coming to Nuisance', p. 566.

[48] See on this rule G. Calabresi and D. Melamed, 'Property Rules, Liability Rules, and Inalienability: One View of the Cathedral' (1972) 85 *Harvard Law Review*, pp. 1115–1123; R. Ellickson, 'Alternatives to Zoning' (1973) *University of Chicago Law Review*, pp. 738–748, as well as R. Epstein, Ch. Gregory and H. Kalven, *Cases and Materials on Torts*, p. 628.

the newcomer knowingly comes to the nuisance; if, in other words, the harm is foreseeable. This, however, does not eliminate the duty of the existing factory to invest in effective preventive measures, wherever possible. Foreseeability is apparently also a criterion in the Norwegian airport cases. The decision that plaintiffs who settled near the airport after it was built were denied compensation by the Norwegian Supreme Court can be understood: they had probably already been compensated because they could purchase their property at a lower price. Thus, this lower price already constituted an *ex ante* compensation for future noise caused by the airport. This only changes if the harm caused through the activities unforeseeably increases. This apparently happened in the Norwegian Hunton Bruk case. The activities had started in 1889 and only in 1957, after the home owners came the area, a new harm causing technology was implemented.

Even the heavily debated French provisions still seem to fit into the economic starting points. Awarding a temporal priority at least has the advantage that it clearly signals to newcomers that they will not be entitled to compensation if the amount of the nuisances meanwhile has not been changed. The French statute in that sense provides incentives to potential victims (but rather also to project developers) to select the location of their projects carefully. Moreover, the protection of the first user disappears from the moment that the nuisance increases, unless this aggravation was foreseeable for the newcomer. Again, this provision aims at providing incentives to newcomers to obtain adequate information not only on the current state of affairs, but also on potential foreseeable changes in the future. The only problem with this type of legislation (or case law) is that the question is not asked to what extent the existing activity could, by using cost-effective precautionary measures, still reduce the nuisance for the neighbours. Since these, moreover, often constitute low transaction cost settings, the fact that the first user can often be the 'cheapest cost avoider' does not necessarily mean that the costs of those preventive measures will then also have to be paid by the first user. If optimal prevention by the first user is the optimal solution, an application of the Coase Theorem, also in this particular situation, shows that parties will bargain in order to implement the most efficient solution. This would even be the case if the newcomers would pay the first user for the implementation of optimal precautionary measures.

5. INDONESIA

This part discusses Indonesia's experience in the use of the 'first use' defence, and takings for public purposes.

5.1. FIRST USE IN INDONESIA

Apparently, the 'first use' defence is relatively unknown in Indonesia. There are no explicit references to the defence in Indonesian textbooks on tort law.[49]

The 'first use' defence can also hardly be found in case law or in statutory provisions. An attempt to use the defence can be found in the Supreme Court ruling on *Handoko Setiono et al v. PT. Radio Zodiac, et al.* In this case, the plaintiffs who lived nearby the premise of PT. Radio Zodiac, a commercial radio station, argued that the radio station's activities constituted an unlawful act against the plaintiffs' interests. The plaintiffs argued that the station was using a building for commercial purposes in a residential area.[50] In addition, the plaintiffs argued that the station's transmitter tower of 100 meter was damaging the plaintiffs' electronic devices and they feared that a lot of damage would be caused if the tower would fall down.[51] An important argument put forward by the defendant, i.e. Radio Zodiac, was that when the tower was erected, the area was still vacant and the plaintiffs were not yet residing there.[52]

Clearly, the defendant attempted to show that by deciding to move close to defendant's premise, the plaintiffs came into nuisance. In the defendant's view, by complaining about the possible impacts of the defendant's tower, which already existed before the plaintiffs moved into the area, the plaintiffs have actually conducted an unlawful act against the defendant's interests.[53]

Apparently, the District Court of Surabaya rejected the defendant's claim. The Court ordered the defendant Radio Zodiac to remove the tower. The Court came to this decision because apparently the permit to erect the tower was procedurally flawed.[54] This ruling was upheld by the Court of Appeal. In addition, the Court of Appeal declared that the defendant's construction permit (*izin mendirikan bangunan*) was void.[55] This decision was confirmed by the Supreme Court.[56] It is important to note that to justify its ruling, the Supreme Court considered that the

---

49 See for example: M.A.M. Djojodirdjo, *Perbuatan Melawan Hukum*, Pradnya Paramita, Jakarta 1979; W. Prodjodikoro, *Perbuatan Melanggar Hukum: Dipandang dari Sudut Hukum Perdata*, Mandar Maju, Bandung 2000; R. Agustina, *Perbuatan Melawan Hukum*, Program Pascasarjana FHUI, Jakarta 2003; and M. Fuady, *Perbuatan Melawan Hukum: Pendekatan Kontemporer*, Bina Cipta Aditya Bakti, Bandung 2010.

50 Supreme Court of Indonesia (2010), Case No. 1097 K/Pdt/2009, *Handoko Setiono et al v. PT. Radio Zodiac, et al.*, p. 2.

51 *Idem*.

52 *Idem*, p. 5, and 15.

53 *Idem*, p. 6.

54 *Idem*, p. 9.

55 *Idem*, p. 10.

56 *Idem*, p. 21.

construction permit to erect the tower was procedurally flawed because it had been issued without the required accompanying nuisance license (*izin gangguan*).[57]

The Court's remark on the *izin gangguan*, also referred to as *izin HO*, i.e. a license derived from the Dutch Indies's *Hinder Ordonantie*, is of high importance to explain the reason not only why the Court rejected the 'first use' defence, but also why there is very limited discussion on the defence. In this regard, the Court relied on the availability of the nuisance permit in order to determine whether the defendant was liable for the plaintiffs' damage. It seems, thus, what matters here is not the question of who was the first user of a resource, but rather the question of whether an injurer has a legal basis, i.e. a permit, to conduct a nuisance. It is also worth mentioning that the Court failed to consider whether the defendant's premise fits in with the local spatial planning.

This conclusion is confirmed by other rulings, in which the determinant factor of liability for a nuisance is the absence of the nuisance license. For example, in Benny William, *et al.*, v. PT. Cahaya Bintan Abadi, *et al.*, the plaintiffs are fishermen who sued companies that had built a port without a nuisance license and an environmental impact assessment (*Amdal*).[58] In this case, the District Court of Tanjung Pinang ruled in favour of the plaintiffs, and ordered the defendant to compensate the plaintiffs as much as IDR 1.47 billion.[59] The decision was upheld by the Court of Appeal,[60] and by the Supreme Court.[61] In other cases, the court ruled that the operation of a rice mill unit without accompanying nuisance license constituted an unlawful act. Hence, the Court required the owners of the milling unit to stop the operation and to move the unit to a location where the owners could obtain the license.[62] Similar reasoning can be found in *Sugiarto v. PT. Multisarimura Indrasarana Tekstil*, where the Court found the defendant liable for operating a coal-fired boiler without nuisance license and without local people's approval. In this case, the Court ordered the defendant to cease the nuisance and to pay compensation as much as IDR 225 million.[63]

In contrast, in *Jemi Rova Basudi, et al. v. PT. Aria Energy Persada, et al.*, the Court argued that the construction and operation of a gas station was based on a licence

---

57 *Idem*.

58 Supreme Court of Indonesia (2012), ruling No. 705 K/Pdt/2011, *Benny William et al., v. PT. Cahaya Bintan Abadi et al.*, at pp. 3–4.

59 *Idem*, at p. 19.

60 *Idem*, at p. 20.

61 *Idem*, at p. 25.

62 See for example: Supreme Court of Indonesia (2007), ruling No. 379 K/Pdt/2003, *Amin Yusuf v. Sarno Bin Ritap*; or Supreme Court of Indonesia (2011), ruling No. 1027 K/Pdt/2011, *Sutajaya, et al. v. Domo*.

63 Supreme Court of Indonesia (2010), ruling No. 1191 K/Pdt /2009, *Sugiarto v. PT. Multisarimura Indrasarana Tekstil (INDRATEKS)*, p. 17.

issued by a relevant authority.[64] The Court refused to examine whether the license had been issued in accordance with the correct procedure. The Court was also rather reluctant to investigate whether the defendant had indeed conducted a nuisance against the plaintiffs. From this ruling, it appears that when the Court found that a nuisance-creating activity had been accompanied by relevant licenses, notably the nuisance license, the injurer could not be held liable.

The importance of the nuisance license or local community's approval in determining liability also indicates an assumption that the injurers always come after the victims. Accordingly, the injurers cannot resort to the 'first use' doctrine. Another explanation for the limited use of the 'first use' defence is the presence of the general obligation not to cause harm to the environment,[65] and the obligation to conduct soil conservation.[66]

Compensation for the installation of an electricity transmission line is an area of law in which an approach similar to the 'first use' doctrine can be found in Indonesia. This is particularly related to the compensation for land owners with respect to the development of high and extra-high voltage transmission lines.

Initially, compensation with respect to the transmission lines was possible according to the Law No. 15 of 1985 concerning electricity. The Law urged the owners of land, buildings, and plants to allow the electricity company to undertake its activities provided that the company would compensate the owners before it would continue with its activities.[67] Later, the obligation to compensate the land owners was, however, limited by the Regulation of the Minister of Mining and Energy No. 01.P/47/MPE/1992. The Regulation stated that land below high and extra-high voltage transmission lines will not be taken over by the electricity company, i.e. *PT. Perusahaan Listrik Negara*,[68] and hence will not be compensated.[69] Similarly, vegetation and buildings that are not located within the safety clearance zone will not be taken and compensated.[70] In other cases compensation hence failed. The land, vegetation, and buildings will be taken and compensated only if they are within the safety clearance zone, or if the area is

64 Supreme Court of Indonesia (2012), ruling No.787 K/Pdt/2012, *Jemi Rova Basudi, et al. v. PT. Aria Energy Persada, et al.*, p. 17.

65 Articles 53 para. 1 and 54 para. 1 of Law No. 32 of 2009 on the protection and management of the environment oblige those who created environmental damage to mitigate and recover the damage. In addition, Article 69 para. 1 of the Law prohibits anybody from creating pollution.

66 Article 15 of Basic Agrarian Law No. 5 of 1960 states that soil conservation is an obligation for those who have a legal relationship with particular land.

67 Article 12 of Law No. 15 of 1985.

68 PT.PLN, a State-owned electricity company.

69 The Regulation of Minister of Mining and Energy No. 01.P/47/MPE/1992, article 5 para. 1.

70 The Regulation of Minister of Mining and Energy No. 01.P/47/MPE/1992, article 5 para. 2.

used for the transmission tower.[71] One court ruling that specifically referred to the 1992 Regulation of the Minister of Mining and Energy is a Supreme Court ruling on *Sugino vs. Pemerintah Republik Indonesia Di Jakarta Cq. Perusahaan Listrik Negara (Persero)* [2008]. In this case, the plaintiff asked for compensating the decrease of property value due to the development of a high voltage transmission line that passed through the plaintiff's property. The Supreme Court upheld the lower court's ruling that rejected the plaintiff's claim. Apparently, in rejecting the plaintiff's claim, the Court relied on the 1992 Regulation of the Minister of Mining and Energy which provided no compensation for land that is not directly used for the transmission tower nor located within the safety clearance zone.[72]

In 1999, the Minister of Mining and Energy issued Regulation No. 975.K/47/MPE/1999 that amended the 1992 Ministerial Regulation. In addition to providing compensation for land used for the transmission tower, the 1999 Regulation also allowed compensation for land, buildings, and vegetation located within the projection of the safety clearance zone or in the area that could hinder the transmission line. Specifically, the 1999 Regulation stated that the compensation is provided for land, buildings, and vegetation that already existed before the development of the transmission line.[73]

Later, in 2009, the Government enacted Law No. 30 of 2009 concerning electricity. The Law allows compensation to be given not only for the land directly used for transmission of electricity, but also for land, buildings, and vegetation passed by the transmission lines to the extent of the decrease of their economic value.[74] Interestingly, the Law clearly states that compensation is not possible for those who intentionally erect buildings and plant vegetation in an area that has been designated for electricity transmission and for which compensation has previously been given.[75]

This recent development, shown in the 1999 Regulation and Law No. 30 of 2009, presents several important aspects. Firstly, the scope of compensation is broadened to include not only land directly used for the location of the transmission tower, but also properties that are affected by the development of transmission lines.[76] Secondly, the compensation is only given for properties

---

71 The Regulation of Minister of Mining and Energy No. 01.P/47/MPE/1992, Article 5 paras. 3 and 4.

72 Supreme Court of Indonesia, Decision No. 1221 K/Pdt/2004, *Sugino vs. Pemerintah Republik Indonesia and PT. PLN (Persero) et al.* [2008], p. 20.

73 The Regulation of Minister of Mining and Energy No. 975.K/47/MPE/1999, article I point 4.

74 Law No. 30 of 2009, Article 30 paras. 1–3.

75 Law No. 30 of 2009, Article 31.

76 One ruling that clearly indicates this aspect is the ruling of High Court of Central Kalimantan on *Dohong Soerapati v. PT. PLN et al* [2013]. In this case, the court ruled that the land owner whose land was passed by a transmission line should be compensated. The court ordered

that existed before the development of transmission lines, and hence, the people who come to the transmission lines afterwards will not be compensated.[77] The latter aspect indicates an approach similar to the 'first use' doctrine. However, as previously indicated, this approach is of limited use in areas other than high-voltage transmission lines.

5.2. TAKINGS IN INDONESIA

Article 33 paragraph 3 of the Constitution states that land, waters, and natural resources are controlled by the State and shall be used to the greatest benefit of the people. According to Wright, this article not only introduces a more socialist perspective to Indonesian land law, but also provides a legal basis for the *eminent domain* because the right to control land is vested in the State.[78] This article is further explained in article 2 paragraph 1 of the 1960 Basic Agrarian Law (BAL), which reiterates the State's power to control land, waters, and natural resources.

Theoretically, takings may take such forms as transfer of title/rights (*pemindahan hak*), land acquisition or relinquishment of rights (*pembebasan tanah atau pelepasan hak*), or the revocation of rights (*pencabutan hak*).[79] Under the transfer of rights, those who have the rights over certain land voluntarily agree to transfer the rights to other parties through, among other ways, the selling of land, land exchange, or land grants.[80] These forms of takings can be found in article 23 of

the electricity company to compensate the land owner by referring to the 1999 Regulation. The company should pay compensation of IDR 209 million. See: High Court of Central Kalimantan, Decision No. No. 31/PDT/2012/PT.PR, *Dohong Soerapati v. PT. PLN et al* [2013], pp. 6–13.

77 In this regard, one could refer to a ruling of the District Court of South Jakarta in *PT. Citra Buana Unggul/PT. Ancol Terang Metal Printing Industri v. PT. PLN (Persero)* [2012] case. The Court referred to both the 1999 Minister Regulation and Law No. 30 of 2009 and concluded that compensation should be given to the owner of properties that had already existed before the development of the transmission. In this case the Court ordered the electricity company to pay compensation as much as IDR 1 billion for the decrease of economic value of the plaintiff's properties due to the company's transmission lines. See: District Court of South Jakarta, Decision No. 639/Pdt.G/2011/PN.Jkt.Sel, *PT. Citra Buana Unggul/PT. Ancol Terang Metal Printing Industri v. PT. PLN (Persero)* [2012], pp. 44–49.

78 G. Wright, 'Indigenous People and Customary Land Ownership under Domestic REDD+ Frameworks: A Case Study of Indonesia' (2011) 7 *Law Environment and Development Journal*, pp. 125–126.

79 S. Setyorini and H. Parwitasari, 'Pemberian Ganti Rugi dalam Rangka Pengadaan Tanah bagi Pembangunan untuk Kepentingan Umum', unpublished paper at Faculty of Law, University of Indonesia, 2013, p. 8.

80 A. Hutagalung, *Tebaran Pemikiran Seputar Masalah Hukum Tanah*, Penerbit LPHI, Jakarta 2005, p. 177.

Presidential Decree No. 55 of 1993 and in article 20 of Presidential Regulation No. 36 of 2005 and No. 65 of 2006.[81]

The process of land acquisition or relinquishment of rights is governed by various provisions under the 1960 BAL. Hutagalung seems to understand land acquisition or relinquishment as a mixture of articles 27, 34, and 40 of BAL which refer to voluntary land acquisition or relinquishment, with article 6 of BAL, which states that all land has a social function.[82] The term 'land acquisition' (*pembebasan tanah*) was initially used to refer to this type of takings, according to the Regulation of the Minister of Home Affairs No. 15 of 1975. The term was subsequently changed into 'relinquishment of rights' (*pelepasan hak*) through Presidential Decree No. 55 of 1993, and Presidential Regulation No. 36 of 2005 and No. 65 of 2006.[83] One important characteristic of this type of takings is the requirement of formal discussion (*musyarwarah*) concerning just compensation for the land owners. According to Law No. 2 of 2012, such a relinquishment of rights shall be carried out by the national land agency.[84]

To avoid arbitrary takings, the Law No. 2 of 2012 defines the types of development projects considered to serve public interest. These include the development of national defence and security, public roads, toll roads, rail lines, dams, harbours, waste treatment facilities, airports, telecommunication lines, oil and gas infrastructure, social facilities, educational infrastructure, government offices, power plants and energy transmission, public markets, and public hospitals.[85]

More importantly, the Law also specifies procedures for land acquisition, including the obligation to provide just compensation. Article 38 of Law No. 2 of 2012 and article 73 of Presidential Regulation No. 71 of 2012 stipulate that if parties cannot settle their disagreement concerning the form and amount of compensation, the land owner has the right to file an appeal with a local district court. The court should come up with a decision regarding the form and amount of compensation within 30 days after it receives the appeal in question. If the land owner disagrees with the court's decision, he/she can appeal to the Supreme Court, which will give its decision in 14 days. Should the land owner disagree with the Supreme Court's decision, the land takers could put the compensation in *konsinyasi*, namely a special account in a district court that will temporarily

81 S. Setyorini and H. Parwitasari, 'Pemberian Ganti Rugi dalam Rangka Pengadaan Tanah bagi Pembangunan untuk Kepentingan Umum'.
82 A. Hutagalung, *Tebaran Pemikiran Seputar Masalah Hukum Tanah*, p. 178.
83 S. Setyorini and H. Parwitasari, 'Pemberian Ganti Rugi dalam Rangka Pengadaan Tanah bagi Pembangunan untuk Kepentingan Umum'.
84 Law No. 2 of 2012, Article 37.
85 Law No. 2 of 2012, Article 10.

keep the compensation so that it will be available should the land owner change his/her mind.[86]

The third type of takings is the revocation of rights. This is stipulated in article 18 of BAL, which states that for the sake of public interest the State can revoke rights over land. However, the article also requires that such a revocation proceeds with just compensation.

The procedure of the three types of takings above should be carefully regulated and controlled. Fitzpatrick observes that during Suharto's regime, State control over land resulted in various conflicts and human rights violations. Such conflicts have occurred especially in relation to the issuance of timber concessions, the designation of protected State forests, and the allocation of land for transmigration projects. It has also led to conflicts due to conflicting claims, namely claims based on customary law against claims based on statutory law.[87] Similarly, with respect to conflicts in the forestry sectors, Segall observes that during Suharto's regime forest resources were egregiously exploited where orders were given from the central Government, and no participation of local communities were allowed.[88] In addition, another terrible example of takings can be seen, for example in the Way Hui case, where the land owners got compensation as little as IDR 5 (0.00032 euro) per m^2.[89] Forced evictions and relocation with very little compensation were also experienced by people of various districts in Central Java whose land was designated for the *Kedung Ombo* dam. In this case, the villagers were offered compensation to the amount of IDR 250–3,000 (0.016–0.192 euro) per m^2.[90]

Clearly, the question of how much compensation should be paid to the property owners is a very important aspect of government takings. Experience during the Suharto regime shows how property owners were often forced to accept very low compensation in the name of development. After the fall of the Suharto regime, some cases indicate that the pendulum swings to the opposite direction, where property owners often ask for compensation according to the actual market price. This new development is also supported by *Masyarakat Profesi Penilai Indonesia* (MAPPI, i.e. the Indonesian association of property appraisers), which has published the guidelines for property appraisal called *Standar Penilaian*

---

86 *Idem*, pp. 10–11.

87 D. Fitzpatrick, 'Disputes and Pluralism in Modern Indonesian Land Law' (1997) 22 *Yale Journal of International Law*, pp. 186–187.

88 C. Segall, 'The Forestry Crisis as a Crisis of the Rule of Law', (2006) 58 *Stanford Law Review*, p. 1553.

89 A. Hutagalung, *Tebaran Pemikiran Seputar Masalah Hukum Tanah*, p. 185.

90 S. Marsoem, W. Adi, and P.G. Manoppo, *Pedoman Lengkap Ganti Untung Pengadaan Tanah: Memetakan Solusi Strategis Pengembangan Infrastruktur Indonesia*, Renebook, Jakarta 2015, pp. 40–41.

Indonesia 306 (SPI 306). Paragraph 5 of the SPI 306 clearly suggests that compensation should be fair and take the market value of property into account.[91] One might predict that the guidelines to play an important role in future property appraisal for development project in Indonesia, since the Law No. 2 of 2012 has required the land agency to use the assessment of property value provided by the appointed appraisers.[92]

Ironically, an example of tacit and illegal takings is still taking place in recent years. This is the compensation mechanism in the aftermath of the Lapindo mudflow in Sidoarjo. Triggered by a series of failures in a gas drilling operated by Lapindo, the mudflow started in 2006. It keeps bursting until now, inundating dozens of villages, forcing thousands of people to abandon their homes, properties, or jobs. In 2010, at least 40,000 people were displaced by the disaster.[93] Amidst the pressure from both the victims and the drilling company, in September 2006 the President issued a Presidential Decree concerning the formation of *Tim Nasional Penanggulangan Semburan Lumpur di Sidoarjo* (Timnas PLS), a Team of Ministers and heads of Government agencies to handle the Sidoarjo mudflow.[94] The team had the responsibility to stop the eruption, manage the mudflow, and handle the resulting social problems.[95] The Decree also stated that the team would initially work for 6 months, and could be prolonged if necessary.[96] One important aspect addressed in this Decree concerns the responsibility of Lapindo. According to the Decree, the establishment of the *Timnas* does not reduce Lapindo's responsibility to control and manage environmental problems and to handle social problems resulting from the mudflow.[97] In addition, the Decree also stated that any expenses needed by the *Timnas* will be covered by Lapindo.[98]

---

91 S. Marsoem, W. Adi, and P.G. Manoppo, *Pedoman Lengkap Ganti Untung Pengadaan Tanah: Memetakan Solusi Strategis Pengembangan Infrastruktur Indonesia*, pp. 543–544. This is an important development because for years land appraisal for development projects in Indonesia has often been based of the so-called *Nilai Jual Objek Pajak* (NJOP, i.e. the sale value of tax object). In most cases the NJOP value is far below the actual market price. This is especially the case for the property in urban area. See: S. Marsoem, W. Adi, and P.G. Manoppo, *Pedoman Lengkap Ganti Untung Pengadaan Tanah: Memetakan Solusi Strategis Pengembangan Infrastruktur Indonesia*, pp. 73–74. See also: M.I. Syah, *Pembebasan Tanah untuk Pembangunan Kepentingan Umum: Upaya Hukum Masyarakat yang Terkena Pembebasan dan Pencabutan Hak*, Permata Aksara, Jakarta 2015, p. 82.

92 Law No. 2 of 2012, Article 34. The Law does not require the appraiser to use particular reference in assessing the value of property. It is likely that the appraiser will then refer to guidelines provided by its association.

93 Anonymous, 'Govt Admits Failure to Pay Compensation for Mudflow Victims', *The Jakarta Post*, 30 May 2010, Available at: www.thejakartapost. com/news/2010/05/29/govt-admits-failure-pay-compensation-mudflowvictims.html.

94 Presidential Decree No. 13 of 2006, Article 1. The structure of the Timnas PLS is defined in Article 2 of the Decree.

95 Presidential Decree No. 13 of 2006, Article 3.

96 Presidential Decree No. 13 of 2006, Article 7.

97 Presidential Decree No. 13 of 2006, Article 5.

98 Presidential Decree No. 13 of 2006, Article 6.

Some major changes have, however, been made through Presidential Regulation No. 14 of 2007 concerning the formation of *Badan Penanggulangan Lumpur Sidoarjo* (BPLS), an agency responsible to undertake tasks previously carried out by the *Timnas*. Hence, it could be concluded that the Regulation has replaced the temporary *Timnas* with a more permanent agency.

Unlike Presidential Decree No. 13 of 2006 which placed financial burdens solely on Lapindo, Presidential Regulation No. 14 of 2007 stated that the Government and Lapindo should share such burdens. This can be shown as follows:

- First, the Presidential Regulation No. 14 of 2007 established a map of affected areas (hereinafter referred to as the 2007 Map).
- Second, the Regulation obliged Lapindo to purchase the properties of the victims located inside the 2007 Map.[99] This type of compensation through land purchase confirmed Lapindo's position which rejected the term 'compensation' since the term was thought to indicate Lapindo's liability for the mudflow. In addition, since the payment was conducted within a sell and purchase of property, the victims' loss of income, let alone their psychological suffering, was by no means compensated. The payments by Lapindo were conducted in two phases of instalments. Initially, Lapindo would pay 20% of the total price, and the remaining 80% of the payments would be paid within 2 years.[100]
- Third, Lapindo would also be responsible for expenses related to the management of embankments and of the Porong River.[101]
- Fourth, Presidential Regulation No. 14 of 2007 stated that compensation for areas outside the affected area of the 2007 Map would be allocated in the national budget.[102]
- Fifth, the Government would also allocate in the national budget expenses related to the management and control of the mudflow.[103]

In 2008, the President issued another regulation, i.e. Presidential Regulation No. 48 of 2008, to amend Presidential Regulation No. 14 of 2007. The 2008 Presidential Regulation maintained all Lapindo's responsibilities specified in the 2007 Presidential Regulation. The most important part of this new Regulation

99 Presidential Regulation No. 14 of 2007, Article 15 para. 1.

100 Presidential Regulation No. 14 of 2007, Article 15 para. 2.

101 Presidential Regulation No. 14 of 2007, Article 15 para. 5. Initially, the mudflow from the embankments was channeled into the Porong River. This initiative has sparked criticism from environmentalist arguing that the channeling of the muddy water will severly damage the River's and eventually the adjacent marine ecosystems. See: J. Schiller, A. Lucas and P. Sulistiyanto, 'Learning from the East Java Mudflow: Disasters Politics in Indonesia' (2008) 85 *Indonesia* 75.

102 Presidential Regulation No. 14 of 2007, Article 15 para 3.

103 Presidential Regulation No. 14 of 2007, Article 15 para 6.

was the inclusion of several villages that by the 2007 Map were considered to be located outside the affected areas. According to the 2008 Presidential Regulation, those villages are Besuki, Pejarakan, and Kedungcangkring.[104] For the victims from these three villages, compensation was paid by the Government, acting as the purchaser of properties located in these villages.[105] It is important to note that the payments by the Government for these three villages would follow the payment by Lapindo for the affected villages of the 2007 Map.[106]

The 2007 Government Regulation underwent a second amendment through Presidential Regulation No. 40 of 2009. There were two important changes arising from this Regulation. First, the 2009 Regulation changed the phases of instalments for the additional villages under the 2008 Regulation into three phases of instalments. The initial instalments were 20% of the total payment for each claim, to be paid out in 2008. Afterwards, 30% of the total payment were paid out in 2009, and the payments for the remaining 50% were to be completed following the completion of Lapindo's payments.[107]

Second, the 2009 Regulation specified three additional villages as areas that will be compensated by the Government. These villages are Siring Barat, Jatirejo, and Mindi.[108] However, unlike the victims residing in the additional villages of the 2008 Regulation, people residing in the additional villages of the 2009 Regulation were not to be compensated through the sell and purchase scheme. Under this new scheme, residents of the three latest additional villages would only receive payments for renting a house for 2 years, living allowances for 6 months, and expenses needed for evacuation.[109] This means that Government inadvertently treated the people from these latest additional villages less favourably compared to the people from the villages specified in the 2008 Regulation.

Third, the 2009 Regulation reduced Lapindo's responsibility by removing its obligation to pay expenses for the management and control of the mudflow.[110] Therefore, all expenses related to the management of the mudflow, including

---

104 Presidential Regulation No. 48 of 2008, Article 15B para 1.

105 Presidential Regulation No. 48 of 2008, Articles 15A and 15B.

106 Similar to Lapindo's payments, compensation for the three villages will be paid out by the Government in two phases of installments. The first installments are 20% of the total payment for each claim, and the remaining 80% will be paid out after Lapindo completes its second installment. See: Presidential Regulation No. 48 of 2008, Article 15A paras 5 and 6. This is quite understandable as the Government expected that the payments for all villages (both outside and inside the affected areas of the 2007 Map) would be completed relatively at the same time.

107 Presidential Regulation No. 40 of 2009, Article 15B, para. 5.

108 Presidential Regulation No. 40 of 2009, Article 15B, para. 1a.

109 Presidential Regulation No. 40 of 2009, Article 15B, para. 9.

110 Presidential Regulation No. 40 of 2009 deletes Article 15 para. 5 of the 2008 Regulation.

the recovery and rehabilitation of its environmental impacts, became the Government's burden.

Initially, Lapindo pledged to provide funds for the evacuation of the victims, emergency shelter, and a house rent assistance package for a two-year term, and a living allowance for nine months. The allocation of these funds can be seen as follows: 5000,000 IDR per family for relocation fund (*uang pindah*), 5 million IDR per family for two-year house rent (*uang kontrak rumah*), and 300,000 IDR per person per month as living allowance (*jatah hidup*).[111]

To implement Presidential Regulation No. 14 of 2007, Lapindo established its subsidiary company, named Minarak Lapindo Jaya (MLJ), which is responsible to carry out the payment and to conduct a sell and purchase agreement on behalf of Lapindo. Following the 2007 Presidential Regulation, the MLJ is obliged to pay compensation under the two phases of instalments, namely a first instalment of 20% of the total price of each claim, and the second instalment of the remaining 80% that would be paid out before the two-year house rent ended. Subsequent to this payment, the victims had to sign a deed of sale (*akte jual beli*) indicating the transfer of the title of the submerged land and buildings to Lapindo.[112]

However, Lapindo still fails to meet its pledges. Until now, there are still some families who have not yet received any compensation by Lapindo. This results in inequality among the victims, by which victims whose payments for land relinquishment are paid by Lapindo suffer more than those whose compensation is paid by the Government. This triggered the Constitutional Court to rule that the payment of compensation by the Government to the victims of the Lapindo mudflow is unconstitutional unless the Government is able to ensure that Lapindo meets its obligation to pay the victims included in the 2007 map.[113]

Regulatory takings have also been examined in the economic analysis of law, from the perspective of the doctrine of eminent domain. It is stressed that the State may have public interest reasons to acquire public property.[114] The State has the choice to either acquire public property by purchasing it or by using the

---

111 Badan Pemeriksa Keuangan Republik Indonesia, 'Laporan Pemeriksaan Penanganan Semburan Lumpur Sidoarjo', 2007, p. 131. Schiller and colleagues also note Lapindo's promise to provide 'other assistance', including: an unemployment wage compensation payment of Rp. 700,000 per month (to 2,288 factory workers, or Rp. 6.2 billion total), relocation compensation to ten factories (Rp. 5.2 billion), other compensation to nine additional factories (Rp. 47.6 billion), and grants to 306 small- and medium-size enterprises (Rp. 4.3 billion). See: J. Schiller, A. Lucas and P. Sulistiyanto, 'Learning from the East Java Mudflow: Disasters Politics in Indonesia' 66.

112 *Idem*, at p. 67.

113 Constitutional Court of Indonesia, decision No. 83/PUU-XI/2013, *Siti Askabul Maimanah, et al. (petitioners)*, 2013, p. 73.

114 S. Shavell, *Foundations of the Economic Analysis of Law*, pp. 110–123.

power of eminent domain. Because obtaining property via purchase may include high bargaining costs there may be advantages for the State to use its powers of eminent domain.[115] Interestingly, economic literature mentions that the aversion of individuals against the risk of takings by the Government should not be the main justification for compensating individuals. The reason given is that in theory individuals could insure against uncompensated takings.[116] However, that may be true in the West where insurance markets are well developed, but not necessarily in the context of a developing country like Indonesia where insurance coverage against uncompensated takings may be largely unavailable. Moreover, Shavell equally indicates that it becomes important to award compensation when the States' motives to take property would be socially inappropriate. There may be many reasons for the State to take possession of property for inappropriate motives, such as salary and status increase for bureaucrats, punishing political opponents or providing benefits to particular interest groups. Precisely for these reasons Shavell argues that a payment requirement can be considered to serve as a beneficial check on takings.[117] This shows that also from an economic perspective, more particularly in the case of Indonesia where (as the examples showed) takings often occur for inappropriate reasons, it is important to award adequate compensation precisely to correct these wrong motives by politicians. And, as was just shown, even in that case adequate compensation is problematic in the case of Indonesia.

6. CONCLUDING REMARKS

This chapter attempted to apply some of the insights from the economic approach to law to specific problems that might arise in the allocation and transfer of land rights in the broad sense. Starting point is that often a variety of conflicts may emerge between various users of land, i.e. holders of property rights over land. As the examples showed these types of conflicts may arise both in the East (in our case the analysis was limited to Indonesia) as well as in the West (Europe and the US), although the specific heading under which those conflicts are defined in the legal system can vary. Depending upon the subject of the conflict, i.e. with whom the conflict especially arises, the conflict could either arise as a problem of 'first use' or 'coming to nuisance' or as a 'regulatory taking'. Common to conflicts in both cases is that there are issues of temporal priority: one user of land right (for example a farmer or other occupant) is the first in time to use particular land rights and others (for example residents or the government) may come later.

[115] S. Shavell, *Foundations of the Economic Analysis of Law*, p. 127.

[116] S. Shavell, *Foundations of the Economic Analysis of Law*, p. 128.

[117] See S. Shavell, *Foundations of the Economic Analysis of Law*, p. 130.

The question we addressed with various examples and from a law and economics perspective is how those temporal issues are and should be dealt with also with a view to an efficient use of the land. The principle of 'first use doctrine' will mostly be used when the conflict arises between two private parties (e.g. a farmer and residences that came to the nuisance). Takings will rather be used when it is the government (hence the term regulatory takings) which uses its sovereign powers to step in in order to intervene in prior land rights.

It was striking to notice that the European and American cases we discussed concerning temporal priority mostly were dealt with under the heading of the 'first use doctrine'.[118] In Indonesia to the contrary, cases with respect to the 'first use doctrine' appeared to be quite limited. This, so we argued, was due to a more general problem related to environmental justice in Indonesia, being that there are serious problems of access to justice for victims of environmental pollution. As a result, many cases are simply not brought to the court. *The Lapindo mudflow* case that was discussed presents a clear example of problems that victims are facing in getting effective access to justice. Courts allow companies largely to rely on permits (based on the old-Dutch Hinder Ordonantie). As soon as the polluter complies with the permit this seems to effectively exclude any liability suit and hence any discussion of 'coming to nuisance'. An intervention in land rights in Indonesia also takes place via regulatory takings. It is, however, often highly doubtful whether, as the law requires, the taking corresponds with a public use. Moreover, many of the takings that occur in Indonesia do not seem to serve the public interest, but rather the private interest of particular strong interest groups. The explanation for many of the takings is often that it rather serves the interests of utility maximizing bureaucrats who are bribed by powerful interest groups as a result of which they set aside rights of existing landowners. This has resulted, especially in the post-Suharto era in holdouts, but also in strong overinvestments (also via takings) by a land mafia, often clearly disregarding traditional land rights and without adequate compensation for the victims who were expropriated.

Those examples once more show that Indonesia is still on a long march towards a true implementation of the rule of law via an accountable and transparent public service. The theoretical starting points concerning the resolution of conflicting land rights as they are proposed in economic analysis and to some extent applied in case law in Europe and in the US (as section 4 showed) remain to a large extent merely theoretical in the case of Indonesia. Access to justice to the (weak) courts remains a dream for many victims of pollution or regulatory takings and conflicts are often decided by a (still) corrupt bureaucracy to the benefit of powerful interest groups (often referred to as a land mafia). Economic analysis can pave the way

118 The scope of this chapter did not allow us to review the literature on regulatory takings in the US and Europe as well.

towards a more effective resolution of conflicting land rights, also in Indonesia, but many structural reforms are still necessary in order to solve those conflicts truly in a way that serves the public rather than private interests.

LAND GRABBING, LAND STRUGGLES AND THE HUMAN RIGHT TO FOOD

Roman HERRE

1. A HISTORIC STARTING POINT

'International Human Rights law is written with the indelible ink made of the blood and sweat of women, men and children who struggle individually or collectively against abuses and for justice.'[1]

The historic reality of this statement is typically underpinned with references to the United States Bill of Rights (1776) and the French Revolution (1789). In the context of the discussion of land struggles and a human right to land, another, older historic event refers more directly to these issues. The so called Great Peasants' War (German: Großer Deutscher Bauernkrieg) was a widespread popular revolt in the German-speaking areas of Central Europe, especially southwestern Germany between 1524 and 1525. It was preceded by more local peasant revolts in the second half of the 15th century like the Bundschuh movement.[2] The historic background of these revolts was the renaissance of Roman law in many parts of Europe – especially Roman property law.[3] In this context, the ruling elites appropriated common lands, forests and waters. The resulting systematic deprivation of access to these resources together with arbitrary corvée has been a key cause for the spreading of rural revolts in Central Europe. In March 1525 representatives of 50 southern German peasant groups (so called Haufen) gathered in Memmingen

1 F. VALENTE, 'Towards the Full Realization of the Human Right to Adequate Food and Nutrition', (2014) 57(2) *Development*, p. 157.

2 W. ZIMMERMANN, *Der große deutsche Bauernkrieg*, deb Verlag Das Europäische Buch, Berlin 1978.

3 D. DAHN, *Wir sind der Staat! Warum Volk sein nicht genügt*, 2013, p. 50; G. SENFT (ed.), *Land und Freiheit – Zum Diskurs über das Eigentum von Grund und Boden in der Moderne*, Promediaverlag, Vienna, 2013, p. 11.

to elaborate a set of demands, the '12 Articles', that can be seen as an articulation of their human rights. Articles 5 and 10 aptly highlight the context of their struggle:

> Article 5:
> 'The high gentlemen have taken sole possession of the woods. If the poor man needs something, he has to buy it for double money. Therefore, all the woods that were not bought (relates to former community woods, which many rulers had simply appropriated) shall be given back to the municipality so that anybody can satisfy his needs for timber and firewood thereof.'
>
> Article 10:
> 'Several have appropriated meadows and acres (community land that was at the disposition of all members), that belong to the municipality. Those we want back to our common hands.'[4]

The uprising against this appropriation and privatization of natural resources ended in a bloody war in 1525, where some 300,000 poorly armed peasants were slaughtered by the soldiers of the aristocracy. This revolt is a relevant but rarely referred to example of social struggle for basic human rights in the context of access to and control over natural resources. It is also a remarkable historic fact that shows that the wave of appropriation of commons[5] – in our case fuelled by the renaissance of Roman property law in Europe – evoked strong opposition by the people as is does today in many parts of the world.

For the contemporary debates on land struggles, this quick look in the history books reminds us of the relation between land conflicts and human rights on the one hand and of the rootedness of human rights in past – and ongoing – social struggles.

Why emphasizing this point? We experience that until the present day all too often the discussions and negotiations on land conflicts and land grabbing are artificially taken out of this context. This results in a systematic exclusion of the proponents of social struggles when it comes to possible answers, policies, initiatives etc. related to these land struggles. On a global level, an interesting example is the Principles for Responsible Agricultural Investment (RAI or PRAI). They have been elaborated as some kind of answer to the ongoing land grabbing by technical experts of the World Bank, the International Fund for Agricultural

4 Translation and inserted comment by Wikipedia, see: https://en.wikipedia.org/wiki/Twelve_Articles, last accessed 10-7-2015.

5 The concept of 'commons' is used here in a broader sense, referring to shared access, reliance, use and governance of natural resource. The Voluntary Guidelines on the Responsible Governance of Tenure of Land, Fisheries and Forests (Tenure Guidelines or TGs) refer to it in Guideline 8.3 as 'publicly-owned land, fisheries and forests that are collectively used and managed (in some national contexts referred to as commons).' They further explain that 'States should where applicable, recognize and protect such publicly-owned land, fisheries and forests and their related systems of collective use and management [...]'.

Development (IFAD), the United Nations Conference on Trade and Development (UNCTAD) and the Food and Agriculture Organisation (FAO). These RAI have evoked protests and resistance among civil society, especially the largest global network of small scale farmers La Via Campesina:

> 'RAI started as an agency-led initiative without participation of the governments of poor countries and of the people affected by such investments: women, peasants/farmers, indigenous peoples, fisherfolks, pastoralists and agricultural workers.'[6]

Such an approach is widespread. The remarkable part of this example, the one well worth to record here, is that the institutions and countries behind the RAI have been seeking legitimacy for these principles through an endorsement by the Committee on World Food Security (CFS). But in 2010 the RAI were rejected by the CFS in its 36th session and the Committee started its own, more inclusive process which ended four years later in 2014 in the adoption of Principles for Responsible Investment in Agriculture and Food Systems (rai).[7] While the content of the two documents will not be discussed here, the changing of the process has been an important case in global policy development. A key underlying reason for this has been the reform of the CFS in 2009, which accepted the role of civil society as a key actor. The CFS reform indeed had the aim of 'making it the foremost inclusive international and intergovernmental platform' dealing with food security, the right to food and nutrition.[8] Under this new CFS, civil society organizations have been 'invited to autonomously establish a global mechanism for food security and nutrition which will function as a facilitating body for CSO/NGOs consultation and participation in the CFS.'[9] The result was the establishment of the Civil Society Mechanism (CSM), a unique self-organized body based on the following principle:

> 'The CSM is an inclusive space open to all civil society organizations, with priority given to the organisations and movements of the people most affected by food insecurity and malnutrition, i.e. smallholder producers, fisherfolk, pastoralists, indigenous, urban poor, migrants, agricultural workers etc. The CSM is founded on the belief that the people most affected by food insecurity and malnutrition must be the agents of their own development, are best placed to represent their own interests and views and are not only victims but also bearers of solutions.'[10]

---

6 Global Campaign for Agrarian Reform 2010 Why We Oppose the Principles for Responsible Agricultural Investment (RAI), available at: www.fian.org/en/news/article/detail/why_we_oppose_the_principles_for_responsible_agricultural_investment/.

7 CFS 2010 Thirty-sixth Session: Final Report, p. 5, available at: www.fao.org/fileadmin/templates/cfs/Docs0910/CFS36Docs/CFS_FINAL_REPORT_REV_w_Annexes_Logos.pdf.

8 CFS 2009 Thirty-fifth Session: Reform of the Committee on World Food Security, available at: www.csm4cfs.org/files/Pagine/2/cfs_reform_doc.pdf.

9 *Ibid.*

10 Civil Society Mechanism web site: www.csm4cfs.org/about_us-2/what_is_the_csm-1/.

Again, this all underpins that human rights and land issues are not an isolated academic or technocratic theme but must be seen and understood as rooted in the people, especially the ones struggling for social justice and equity. And history shows that such struggles have ever since embarked on the land question.

1.1. ONGOING SOCIAL STRUGGLES

In consequence, human rights based approaches to land must inherently be rooted in the existing social struggles and its protagonists, the rural social movements like organizations of peasants, landless farmers, rural youths, rural women, indigenous peoples, pastoralists, fisherfolks and others. On a global level this can be done, among other ways, by taking serious account of the documents, statements, and demands of these groups in the context of policy discussions. The following list provides some key examples of the more recent demands and declarations related to the land question.

- Land, Territory and Dignity Forum: For a New Agrarian Reform based on Food Sovereignty! (Porto Alegre, 2006).[11]
- Declaration of the Forum for Food Sovereignty (Nyéléni, 2007).[12]
- Synthesis report of the Forum for Food Sovereignty (Mali, Nyéléni, 2007).[13]
- The Kimberley Declaration: International Indigenous Peoples Summit on Sustainable Development (Khoi-San Territory, Kimberley, South Africa, 2002).
- World Charter for the Right to the City (Social Forum of the Americas, Quito, 2004 / World Urban Forum, Barcelona, 2004 / World Social Forum, Porto Alegre, 2005 / Revision in preparation for Barcelona, 2005).
- What's missing from the climate talks? Justice! (Bali 2007).[14]
- Dakar Appeal against Land Grabbing (World Social Forum, Dakar 2011).[15]
- Rights to Water and Land, a Common Struggle. Dakar to Tunis: Declaration of the Global Convergence of Land and Water Struggles (World Social Forum, Tunis 2015).[16]

---

11 FAO 2009, Annex 1.
12 FAO 2009, Annex 2.
13 FAO 2009, Annex 3.
14 FAO 2009, Annex 7.
15 Www.fian.org/fileadmin/media/publications/Dakar_Appeal_en.pdf.
16 Http://viacampesina.org/en/images/stories/pdf/2015-04-Dakar%20to%20Tunis%20Declaration_EN_finalfinal.pdf.

Common to most of these documents is the holistic approach to land and natural resources, including issues of social reproduction and democratisation of control over these resources, as confirmed by the most recent declaration:[17]

> 'Our solidarity, grounded in our commitment as activists, is built upon the following principles and convictions that unify our struggles:
>
> 1. That the human rights to water, food and land are fundamental, and crucial for life. All people, men, women, adults, children, rich, poor, rural and urban dwellers, are entitled to them.
>
> 2. That water and land are not only vital natural resources, but are also part of our common heritage, whose security and governance must be preserved by each community for the common good of our societies and the environment, now and for future generations.
>
> 3. Water, land and seeds are Commons, and not commodities.
>
> [...]
>
> 5. Land water management policies should promote the achievement of social justice, gender equality, public health and environmental justice.'

2. CONTEXTUALIZING LAND GRABBING

Land grabbing became an emerging global policy issue around 2007. But what exactly is land grabbing? This question has been widely debated in academic and policy circles.[18] While there have been numerous efforts to define land grabbing, Künnemann and Monsalve point out that the definition, understanding and particular framing of land grabbing varies significantly. It mainly depends on who is doing the framing, and for what purpose.[19] Consequently, this means that we have to deal with an array of definitions and views on land grabbing. In this tangle of definitions a human rights framework is very helpful for assessing and understanding these definitions and their origins.

Nonetheless it is widely accepted that land grabbing is not really a new phenomenon but the latest rush for land and related resources like water and forests. It is likewise understood that this latest rush has its own and distinct features worth taking a closer look at.

---

17 *Ibid.*

18 See for example: BMZ, *Investments in Land and the Phenomenon of Land Grabbing. Challenges for Development Policy*, BMZ Strategy Paper, 2/2012; S. Borras, J. Franco, 'Global land grabbing and trajectories of agrarian change: a preliminary analysis' (2012) 12(1) *Journal of Agrarian Change*, pp. 34–59; L. Cotula 'The international political economy of the global land rush: a critical appraisal of trends, scale, geography and drivers' (2012) 39(3–4) *The Journal of Peasant Studies*, pp. 649–680; M.E. Margulis, N. McKeon, S.M. Borras 'Land grabbing and global governance: critical perspectives' (2013) 10(1) *Globalizations*, pp. 1–23.

19 R. Künnemann, S. Monsalve, 'International Human Rights and Governing Land Grabbing: A View from Global Civil Society' (2013) Vol. 10, No. 1 *Globalizations*, p.124.

2.1. ... A CONVERGENCE OF MULTIPLE CRISES

First and foremost, this latest rush must be seen in the context of multiple global crises: The climate crisis, the food price crisis, the energy (or fuel) crisis, the resource crisis and the financial crisis. Different types of powerful actors respond to those crises. Without being exhaustive, some key responses are:

- Finance capital (including banks, investment companies, hedge funds, pension schemes ...) seeks for new and supposedly safer investment frontiers and models;
- Governments and a growing segment of the broader economy seek a transition from a fossil-based to a bio-based economy, which implies a huge additional demand for land.[20] The most prominent example is the global agro fuel expansion and the related (mostly national) policies promoting the expansion;
- Proponents of land grabbing (they rather call it large scale land investments) push for positive, facilitating, supportive frameworks for those investments (e.g. G8 Land Transparency Initiative,[21] Benchmarking Business in Agriculture,[22] Farmland Principles ...);[23]
- Agrifood businesses and some States seek to secure their supply of food and feedstuff via direct control over land (they call it vertical integration of businesses).

These responses are 'land-demanding'. They create or increase the interest of these actors in controlling land and related natural resources. In this context of crisis, scholars specify that land grabbing is a 'response to the convergence of [these] multiple crises'.[24]

---

20 This process is possibly spearheaded by productive capital ('real economy') and followed/reinforced by financial capital. See Clapp, 'Financialization, Distance and Global Food Politics' (2013) 41(5) *The Journal of Peasant Studies*, p.3.

21 Later renamed as land partnership, see www.donorplatform.org/land-governance/g8-land-partnerships accessed 11-10-2014.

22 See for example the presentation of IFC, World Bank: http://de.slideshare.net/riatenorio/augusto-and-grahame-ppt accessed 12-11-2014.

23 Www.unpri.org/areas-of-work/implementation-support/the-principles-for-responsible-investment-in-farmland/.

24 S. Borras, J. Franco, S. Gómez, C. Kay and M. Spoor, 'Land grabbing in Latin America and the Caribbean' (2012) 39(3–4) *The Journal of Peasant Studies*, p. 851; P. McMichael, 'The land grab and the corporate food system restructuring' (2012) 39(3–4) *The Journal of Peasant Studies*, p.681.

2.2. ... OF CASES AND STRUCTURES

A vast body of literature and documentation today shows that the enforcement of these particular interests is accompanied by violations of human rights and frequently by brutal evictions and conflicts over land and water with the existing local population, the existing land users. Later on, a closer look will be taken at one such cases in Cambodia.

On the other hand, less attention is given to the underlying deep structural transformation of land grabbing. A fast track concentration of land in the hands of a small number of actors is one of the defining structural features. For example 1,087 documented cases of land grabbing by one internet platform comprise some 40 Million hectares of land.[25] This relates to an average land size of 36,800 hectares of each case.

Furthermore, the local population and local land users do not play a role at all in this 'total rural transformation'.[26] The World Bank's framing of the issue underpins this ignorance. In its 2011 flag ship publication on land grabbing the bank proposes among other things the expansion of maize cultivation on 148 million hectares land globally that has a 'low population density'.[27] They calculate some 10 jobs for 1,000 hectares prospecting 1.48 million jobs globally.[28] Following the bank's own numbers some 11.7 million people – almost a tenfold number – actually sustain their livelihood on those 148 million hectares. The report does not provide any answer to the question of what will happen with them. And it does not discuss whether these 'development' plans are in the interest of these 148 million people living in 'not so densely populated' rural areas.

Lastly, scholars point to the fact that land grabbing has to be seen in the context of the financialization of the food systems.[29, 30] Following Epstein, financialization

---

25 Land Matrix at: www.landmatrix.org/en/ accessed 11-10-2014. For a critique on the global statistics on land grabbing see M. Edelman, 'Messy hectares: questions about the epistemology of land grabbing data' (2013) 40(3) *The Journal of Peasant Studies*, pp. 485–501.

26 Joaqium Lira Maia, large scale land owner and member of the state parliament of Para in Brazil. Quoted from the TV documentary: ZDF zoom 2015, Täter oder Wohltäter. Die Macht der Agrarriesen.

27 World Bank 2011, pp. 39, 172, 173.

28 Murray Li questions the World Banks job calculation as too optimistic. See T. Murray Li, 'Centering labor in the land grab debate' (2011) 38(2) *The Journal of Peasant Studies*, pp. 281–298). It should also be taken into consideration that especially the jobs in the agricultural sector are often seasonal, precarious and badly payed. See for example Misereor, FIAN, IUF (2014) *Harvesting Hunger. Plantation Workers and the Right to Food*, available at: www.fian.org/es/biblioteca/publicacione/detail/harvesting_hunger_plantation_workers_and_the_right_to_food/.

29 R. Isakson, 'Financialization and the Transformation of Agro-food Supply Chains: A Political Economy' (2013) Yale University International Conference: Food Sovereignty: A Critical Dialogue, Conference Paper #9, available at: www.yale-university.org/agrarianstudies/foodsovereignty/pprs/9_Isakson_2013.pdf; Clapp, 2013.

30 Within the dominant discourses the term food system tends to be reduced to international trade, quantities of global food production and retailer based distribution. This ignores the multifaceted realties of food production, distribution and consumption. Thus food systems (local, national, global) should be understood based on a holistic view encompassing

of agriculture and food systems can be defined as the 'increasing importance of financial markets, financial motives, financial institutions, and financial elites in the operation of the economy and its governing institutions, both at national and international level'.[31] In the past, the majority of agribusiness companies and financial investors refrained from participating in agricultural production itself. For them, the economic environment and risks of farming had been too high (low producer prices, bad harvests …). Intense concentration happened upstream and downstream the value chain: in the input market (seeds, fertilizer and agrochemicals), trade, processing and retail.[32] The concentration process in the global food system largely ignored farming itself. Now as prices for food rise and market opportunities multiply (bio economy, agro fuels, flex crops[33] …) they enter and see land as one of the last investment frontiers for the financial world. This implies a commodification of land where its narrow economic value becomes dominant which inherently cuts off the social, cultural, ecological, historic or territorial values and aspects.

This essay puts a special emphasis on a dual perspective on land grabbing, seeing land grabbing from a case by case perspective and as a global structural process and phenomenon. As will be made clear, this double perspective allows addressing relevant questions that are less discussed in this context. As some structural aspects have been discussed above, concrete cases will be addressed now.

3. LAND STRUGGLES: THE CASE OF CAMBODIA'S 'BLOOD SUGAR'

> 'They burned everything … including the rice. They didn't allow us to harvest first. They said they wanted to grow sugarcane. They destroyed our houses so they could grow sugarcane' (Widow, Oddar Meanchey province, October 2011).[34]

---

food production (including e.g. systems of seed reproduction and access to land/ land concentration), distribution (including informal systems, religious systems, inter-household distribution and local markets), social relations, enabling and disabling policies (subsidies, trade policies, public investments …) and cultural aspects. From a right to food perspective, the food system can be seen as the social construct that affects the realization of the right to food including all aspects of normative content of the right to food.

31 G. Epstein, 'Introduction', *Financialization and the World Economy*, Edward Elgar, Cheltenham 2005.

32 For an overview of the existing concentration see: Econexus, Bern Declaration 2013 Agropoly. Available at: www.econexus.info/sites/econexus/files/Agropoly_Econexus_BerneDeclaration.pdf.

33 Further reading on flex crops: B. McKay et al 2014 The Politics of Sugarcane flexing in Brazil and beyond, available at: https://www.tni.org/en/publication/the-politics-of-sugarcane-flexing-in-brazil-and-beyond-0.

34 *Equitable Cambodia, Inclusive Development International* (2013) Bittersweet Harvest: A Human Rights Impact Assessment of the European Union's Everything But Arms Initiative

In the last few years the Government of Cambodia granted some 150,000 hectares of land as Economic Land Concessions (ELCs) to private companies for agro-industrial sugarcane production.[35] The rapidly expanding sugar industry has been accompanied by serious and systematic human rights violations. People have been forcibly evicted and their property destroyed; they lost access to their land, water and their self-determination; they have been criminalized and denied access to justice. Women and children were disproportionally affected. These violations result in destructions of rural livelihoods, loss of income and overall impoverishment of villagers.

The development of the Cambodian sugar industry is subjected to numerous local liabilities infringements, which include the national Land Law (2001) for the protection of tenure rights and the Sub-Decree #146 on Economic Land Concessions (2005) containing safeguards to mitigate risks associated with expulsions, etc. For example, many ELCs exceed the maximum allowed size of 10,000 hectares and/or ignore provisions that sharply restrict involuntary resettlements or provisions on consultations with the local population before granting ELCs.

3.1. THE KAMPONG SPEU SUGAR CANE CONCESSIONS

In February 2010, the Cambodian Government approved two side-by-side ELCs in Thpong and Aoral districts, Kampong Speu Province, for the companies Phnom Penh Sugar PPS (~9,000 ha) and Kampong Speu Sugar KSS (~9,000 ha). The companies are owned by the Cambodian tycoon Ly Yong Phat and his wife.[36] In March 2011 Prime Minister Hun Sen signed a sub-decree allowing land in the Aoral Protected Area to be reclassified and KSS concession to be expanded by 4,700 hectares. Today the consolidated twin concession is totalling over 23,000 hectares of land.[37]

Recent information showed that the Australian ANZ Bank, the third largest bank in Australia, has financed PPS with 40 million USD.[38] ANZ is a signatory to the Equator Principles, a global ethical banking code and has been awarded as the most sustainable bank by the Dow Jones Sustainability Index.[39]

in Cambodia, available at: www.inclusivedevelopment.net/wp-content/uploads/2013/10/Bittersweet_Harvest_web-version.pdf, 2013, p.1.

35 LICADHO Land Concession: Crops, available at: www.licadho-cambodia.org/land_concessions/ accessed 22-5-2015.

36 Furthermore, both companies are subsidiaries of the L.Y.P. Group. See: www.lypgroup.com/download/lyp-group-brochure.pdf, accessed 22-5-2015.

37 *Equitable Cambodia*, 2013, p.27.

38 Inclusive Development International (22 January 2014) 'ANZ bankrolls massive land grab in Cambodia', www.inclusivedevelopment.net/anz-bankrolls-massive-land-grab-in-cambodia/ accessed 22-5-2015; and www.abc.net.au/pm/content/2014/s4102199.htm, accessed 22-5-2015.

39 This includes the highest ranking in the social dimension. See: www.sustainability-indices.com/review/industry-group-leaders-2013.jsp, accessed 22-5-2015.

Back in 2007, villagers and local authorities disagreed with a first request to cooperate with the company. In 2009 company staff came back and just informed the villagers that they would clear the forests while the rice fields would remain untouched. Around 300 villagers protested against these activities; they went to the company site and the commune council, demanding the formal acknowledgement of their legal possession rights before the company started clearing land. While this demand was ignored, the company also started to destroy rice fields and houses in 2010. The villagers collected 1,350 thumbprints for a petition against this project.[40] ... In March 2010 they also blocked a main road.

To get control of the land, the company used tricks, intimidation and forced evictions. Villagers unable to read were lured to thumb-print documents handing over their land while being told by the Commune Chief it was to construct a road, map their land rights or even a petition to contest the sugar company project (sic). Other villagers were bullied and coerced into accepting so-called 'compensations offers' proposed by the authorities on behalf of the concessionaires – sometimes never receiving the money. Villagers of O'Ang Khum were proposed unacceptable low compensation: US$ 200/ha for their rice fields, US$ 100/ha for other land.[41] Those 'compensation offers' were reportedly accompanied by notions like 'if you don't accept you will get nothing. We will still take the land' or if you don't accept 'you will get air instead.'[42] Eleven Trapaing Prolet households received a combined total of US$ 2,265, with individual payments ranging from US$ 15 to 500 for the loss of their homes, land and crops, as well as moving costs. Some farmers in this area received replacement land plots ranging from 0.156 ha to 3 ha.[43]

> 'There were no meetings. There were no compensation negotiations. We were forced. We did not want to sell our land for such a low price' (Kork villager).[44]

One village, Pis was completely destroyed. With no prior notice and no court order, residents learned about the sugar concessions when company bulldozers and about 30 soldiers armed with guns and stun batons arrived to clear their land and demolish their homes in February 2010.[45] The military troops deployed to protect the company's land clearances have direct financial links to the company. Some villagers have been resettled to plots too small to produce enough food (0.2 ha) and on land very difficult to farm (rocky and sandy soil). Some have received cash compensation ranging from US$ 20 to 900.[46]

---

40 *Equitable Cambodia*, 2013, p. 80.
41 *Ibid.*, p. 56.
42 *Ibid.*, pp. 52, 56, 75.
43 *Ibid.*, p. 64.
44 *Ibid.*, p. 51.
45 *Ibid.*, p. 53.
46 *Ibid.*, p. 64.

Many families lost *access to agricultural land*. Overall the concession has been documented as encroaching on more than 2,000 hectares of farmland belonging to approximately 1,100 families in fifteen villages in Amlaing commune in Thpong district, and Trapaing Chor commune in Aoral district. For most of the affected people the land taken by the company was ancestral land.[47]

> 'It was my land – it has been in my family since the time of my ancestors. Now everything is gone.' (O'Pralov villager)[48]

Community forests, essential for activities such as grazing, gathering fruits, herbs and medicine, and wood collecting, were also destroyed. Amliang Community Forest and Taleo Community Forest, totalling 1,805 ha were completely cleared, while villagers estimate that an additional 1,000 ha of forests were also destroyed within the concession boundaries.[49] Destruction of community forests in the north-western part of Trapaing Chor commune (Srea'kin village) was ongoing until 2013.

Access to water has also been eroded as local water resources have been blocked (for instance with dams), polluted or depleted by the company to meet plantation requirements. Sugar mill processes and agricultural inputs have contaminated water resources, so many people and livestock can no longer access these sources for drinking and household use without getting sick. Residents of Snoul, O'Ang Khum, Kork, and O'Pralov also lost fishing resources, and can no longer find edible water plants such as morning glory and lily that used to grow locally.[50]

> 'Everything is gone. The forest and fishing areas are gone.' (Trapaing Prolet villager)[51]

In addition, the company built a dam for irrigation in 2014. This dam blocked the small river to La'ngim village so that water scarcity was exacerbated.[52]

Despite military and police intimidation, community representatives succeeded in having the Government returning some 1,000 hectares to several villages. However, the size of land returned was far less than what the villagers owned and used before the company came.[53]

---

47 *Ibid.*, p. 27.
48 *Ibid.*, p. 58.
49 *Ibid.*, p. 59.
50 *Ibid.*
51 *Ibid.*
52 Interviews and site visits in June 2014.
53 *Equitable Cambodia*, 2013, p. 80.

3.2. THE ROLE OF THE EUROPEAN UNION

The trade initiative 'Everything But Arms' (EBA) was adopted in 2001 by the European Union (EU) against the backdrop of the Millennium Development Goals, which emphasized 'aid for trade'. Designed with the explicit intention of promoting development in the world's poorest countries, the initiative grants full duty-free and quota-free access to the European market for the 49 countries classified as Least Developed Countries (LDCs) – including Cambodia. Market access for sugar was fully liberalized by October 2009, which is especially relevant as the EU guarantees a minimum sugar price higher than the world market price. In 2012 for example the price for one ton of raw sugar has been approximately € 175 (or 50%) higher per ton within the EU market.[54]

The logic of the EBA initiative, according to its proponents, is that increased trade fosters economic growth, job creation and consequentially, poverty reduction. It is asserted that the provision of preferential tariffs stimulates international investment, promotes industrialization and diversification of their economies.[55] Data shows that EBA has been indeed 'successful' by fuelling a boom in Cambodian sugar industries and their exports to the EU (see Table 1). According to the companies involved in sugar cane plantations, EBA has been a primary motivation for their land acquisitions and operations in Cambodia.[56] Whereas in 2006 sugar cane holdings were negligible, Cambodia now has roughly 150,000 hectares of land under agro-industrial sugar cane production.

Table 1. Development of Cambodian sugar exports to the EU[57]

	2008	2009	2010	2011	2012	2013
Total sugar exports to EU, in thousands of dollars	28	51	3,851	13,229	10,614	51,615[58]
Sugar exports to EU compared to total sugar exports, in percentage	6.5%	30%	90%	94%	100%	–
Sugar exports to EU, in tons	–	–	10,000	22,500	15,501	64,917

The surge in exports undeniably had a significant impact upon the Cambodian economy and people. While a few elites profit from the sugar industry, thousands of the country's poorest families were forcibly deprived from land access – the basis for their livelihoods. From August 2010 on, civil society, including the local communities, formally and repeatedly expressed concern towards the EU over

54 Own calculation based on European Commission: DG AGRI (2013) Sugar Price Reporting.
55 *Equitable Cambodia*, 2013, p. 19.
56 *Ibid*, p. 22.
57 Hands off the Land Alliance (2014) Case Dossier: Cambodia. Sugar cane plantations, human rights violations and EU's 'Everything But Arms' initiative, available at: https://www.fian.de/publikationen/shop-mediathek/artikel-details/?tt_products[cat]=10&tt_products[product]=108 2014, p. 7.
58 Converted from Euro 38,390 thousand.

EBA as a driver of land grabbing and human rights violations in the agro-industrial sector.[59] In September 2012 the affected communities directly demanded from Trade Commissioner Karel de Gucht to 'stop the discrimination against the sugar affected/evicted communities' and 'immediately investigate on the situation' in terms of human rights violations. They also demanded a temporary suspension of EBA trade preferences, at least for sugar.[60]

As Surya Subedi, the UN Special Rapporteur on the Situation of Human Rights in Cambodia stated, 'in general, it is not clear to what extent the people of Cambodia have actually benefited from land concessions.'[61] A 2007 report of the United Nations Office of the High Commissioner for Human Rights concludes even more explicit: 'Instead of promoting rural development and poverty reduction, economic land concessions have compromised the rights and livelihoods of rural communities in Cambodia.'[62]

3.3. RIGHTFUL RESISTANCE

Resistance strategies of the local communities have been plenty. Apart from the ongoing interaction with the EU, some key aspects of the struggles shall be mentioned here:

- Engaging with local authorities: tabling the land grab at the commune council.
- Action research: affected communities themselves documented violations of human rights and overall activities of the land grabbers and local authorities. This included discussing the latest developments and own strategies.
- Protest and demonstrations (local and in Phnom Penh).
- Open resistance: community members blocked bulldozers destroying houses and forests. They also blocked a national road and set a small hut for machinery on fire.
- Grassroots networking: quarterly meetings of most sugar cane affected communities in Cambodia are being organized to exchange and align strategies.
- Alliances with national and international NGOs: With this support they could address the investments of international banks (Deutsche Bank in Koh

59 In August 2010 a first letter was addressed to Mr. Rafael Dochao Moreno, Charge d'Affairs of the EU Delegation to Cambodia, followed by multiple letters to EU Commissioner De Gucht.

60 Letter of the 10 community representatives of the communities affected by the sugar cane land grabs in the three provinces, dated September 2012.

61 UN doc. A/HRC/21/63/Add.1/Rev.1, 11 October 2012, Report of the Special Rapporteur on the situation of human rights in Cambodia, Surya P. Subedi, Addendum, A human rights analysis of economic and other land concessions in Cambodia, p. 3.

62 United Nations Office of the High Commissioner for Human Rights (2007) Economic Land Concessions in Cambodia: A Human Rights Perspective, p. 1.

Kong and ANZ in Kampong Speu) and the responsibilities of international institutions like the European Union.

The land grabbers on the other hand, used multiple methods to silence and minimize resistance:

- They organized support from state authorities (police and military – battalion 313).
- Local authorities have been pushed not to intervene (a typical answer to villagers complains has been 'there is no solution for the problem')
- Courts have been used to criminalize people trying to resist.
- Community leaders were arbitrary detained.
- Community leaders were strategically 'employed' by the company (2012, 2014). This substantially weakened the resistance.[63]
- Selective (and hidden) payment of 'compensation' silenced key persons in the community.

4. LAND STRUGGLES: UNDERLYING POWER IMBALANCES

An emblematic case related to the issue of power imbalances in land struggles is the Barro Blanco hydro dam project in Panama. Loans to the large scale hydro dam project have been provided by three development banks, the German Investment Corporation (DEG), the Dutch Development Finance Company (FMO) and the Central American Bank for Economic Integration (CBIE). Total funding from the three banks amounts to US$78 million.[64]

The Ngöbe-Buglé indigenous community affected by the project argued that the Barro Blanco dam will affect part of their indigenous territory and cause the flooding of their homes, schools and religious, archaeological, and cultural sites. Despite existing national and international human rights obligations, the Panamanian Government, GENISA and the banks failed to obtain the free, prior, and informed consent (FPIC) of the Ngöbe-Buglé before the project was approved.

A report by the panel of the DEG – FMO Independent Complaint Mechanism found that both development banks violated their own policies by failing to adequately assess the risks to indigenous rights and the environment before approving a US$50 million loan to GENISA, the developer of the Barro Blanco

[63] After a community spokesperson changed sides, one villager explained 'We feel like a ship floating on a large sea without a pilot'.

[64] Website of CBIE: www.bcie.org/?prj=35&title=Generadora%20del%20Istmo.%20Proyecto%20Hidroel%E9ctrico%20Barro%20Blanco&lang=es#.VbHvovl3uBE accessed 24-7-2015.

project.[65] The panel found that the 'lenders should have sought greater clarity on whether there was consent to the project from the appropriate indigenous authorities prior to project approval'.

After eight years of protests and local opposition, the Autoridad National del Ambiente (ANAM) announced a temporary suspension of the project in February 2015. This seemed to be a big success for the local communities. But the lenders answered this action with an explicit intervention and pressured the Government to proceed with the dam project.

> 'As lenders of the Barro Blanco Project, but more importantly, as lenders to projects in Panama in general, we fear that actions such as the one taken against GENISA may weight upon future investment decisions, and harm the flow of long-term investments in Panama. We ask the relevant authorities, including ANAM, to take prompt actions in search of reaching a favourable agreement by all stakeholders involved in the Barro Blanco Project.'[66]

This letter can indeed be interpreted as blackmail by powerful development banks.[67] While it is impossible to detail the impact of this letter, it is a fact that shortly afterwards, in May 2015, the project was resumed. This case exemplifies the power imbalance between development agents (here development banks) and local communities that struggle for their human rights.

5. CONTEMPORARY LAND STRUGGLES: COMPLEX AND MULTI-LAYERED

As the two examples already indicate, struggles for land and territories by affected communities and rural social movements are very complex. The underlying land conflicts and related violations of human rights are the result of a range of structural and contextual factors, including:

- Highly unequal power structures.
- Overly market oriented economic development policies (including commodification of land).
- Elitist (non-democratic) decision making processes.

---

65 Report of 29 May 2015 of the Panel of the FMO-DEG Complaints Mechanism, available at: https://www.deginvest.de/DEG-Documents-in-English/About-DEG/Responsibility/Barro_blanco_final_report_EN.pdf last accessed 23-7-2015.

66 Unpublished and undated letter from FMO, DEG and CBIE to the Vice-president of Panama and Minister of External Affairs.

67 Www.swr.de/report/entwicklungshilfe-auf-kosten-der-ureinwohner-ein-von-deutschland-finanzierter-staudamm-bedroht-stammesgebiete-in-panama/text-des-beitrags-entwicklungshilfe-auf-kosten-der-ureinwohner/-/id=233454/did=15702582/mpdid=15723554/nid=233454/jr01cd/index.html.

- Weak, corrupt and inefficient land administration institutions (including both traditional and State institutions).
- Discrimination in access to justice.
- Abuse of power by non-State actors.
- Persecution (criminalization) of human rights defenders and organized social movements struggling for access to land and natural resources.

Moreover, the simple dichotomy of land conflicts involving a land lord and a local village/community certainly does not reflect reality (any more). Mostly a complex mix of actors is involved from national elites to international funders or lenders, from farm management companies to investment funds and often involving a cascading structure of primary, secondary, tertiary etc. investors. Also the affected communities mostly are not a homogenous group. For instance, some people, like local chiefs, benefit from land acquisition and support this process. Others, typically the more marginalized people of the community and the ones more dependent on community forests etc. strongly oppose a land grab.

This complexity is also about multiple political arenas in which the struggle takes place. It can involve the local authorities, national and external governments, arenas of transnational corporations,[68] national as well as international courts like the Inter-American Court of Human Rights.[69] As we will see later, it can also involve different international governance instruments with their associated institutions, like the World Bank Inspection Panel, the OECD Guidelines for Multinational Corporations and their national contact points or monitoring Committees and Special Procedures of the international human rights system.

These two aspects relate to a third one, the geographic dimension of social struggles. Some struggles focus on local change (e.g. give back stolen land), some try to incorporate a change in the national legislation in their struggles and still others might try to change the structure of the global political support for land grabs (e.g. the struggle of La Via Campesina started in the 1990s against the Word Trade Organization under the slogan 'WTO and IMF: OUT!').

This complexity implies opportunities as well as problems. Opportunities can be that local communities are able to find allies in other counties, from sporadic interaction to strategic international alliances. Others use this for a strategical 'leap-frogging', where they can use international fora and then come back to

68 For example the annual general meeting of German TNCs is frequently being used as a platform for struggles against human rights abuses. For more information, see for example the work of the Association of Ethical Shareholders Germany at www.kritischeaktionaere.de/englishlanguage.html.

69 See for example the case of the indigenous community Sawhoyamaxa vs the State of Paraguay. Inter-American Human Rights Court, Sawhoyamaxa vs Paraguay, Corte IDH. Caso Comunidad Indígena Sawhoyamaxa vs Paraguay. Decision of 29 March 2006. Series C No. 146, par. 140, at www.corteidh.or.cr/pais.cfm?id_Pais.

their local struggles with support.[70] This can be the case when for example the Committee on Economic, Social and Cultural Rights condemns State actions in their concluding observations, as in a case of land grabbing in Uganda.[71] It can also be related to global norm setting processes, where for example the negotiation of the UN Land Tenure Guidelines (see the next section) set new norms for States that now can be used as a monitoring tool by civil society.

New problems come up when agricultural and land investments are done more and more through complex investments constructs, often including tax and regulation havens out of reach. In effect these constructs blur concrete responsibility and issues of accountability. Clapp refers to this as a 'distancing of accountability'.[72]

In this quite confusing arena, it is paramount for the affected people and possible allies to strategically choose the right entry point(s). The following section will include a discussion on such an approach based on human rights.

6. LAND GRABBING AND THE HUMAN RIGHT TO ADEQUATE FOOD

> 'The challenge is how human rights can better support the struggles of those fighting for their human dignity and move the pendulum towards an equitable and sustainable societal model and food system, which has the promotion and realization of all human rights for all at the center [...]'.[73]

The human right to food is enshrined in the Universal Declaration of Human Rights (1948, Article 12) and the Covenant on Economic, Social and Cultural Rights (1966, Article 11). The UN Committee on Economic, Social and Cultural Rights (CESCR) adopted the authoritative interpretation of the Right to Food in 1999 though General Comment No. 12. In 2004 the members of the FAO have adopted the Voluntary Guidelines for the Progressive Realization of the Right to Food (VG RtF). Today, these documents are the key references for discussing the Right to Food and help understanding the link between land and the human right to adequate food.

---

70 M. Edelman, C. James, 'Peasants' rights and the UN system: quixotic struggle? Or emancipatory idea whose time has come' (2011) 38(1) *The Journal of Peasant Studies*, p. 91.

71 For a summary of the related case and the concluding observations of the UN-Committee see: www.fian.org/news/article/detail/uganda_urged_to_give_land_back_to_mubendes_evicted_community/ accessed 17 July 2015.

72 Clapp, 2013.

73 Valente, 2014.

6.1. ACCESS TO LAND AND THE RIGHT TO FOOD

As detailed in the legal documents referred to above, access to land and natural resources is a key component of the right to food from multiple perspectives. CESCR General Comment No. 12 possibly provides the best starting point for understanding the normative relation between land and food. It first highlights that 'feeding oneself directly from productive land or other natural resources' is a key element of availability of food for a person.[74] Second, access to land and natural resources provides the basis for economic activities of the vast majority of the rural population in the global south. They sell products from the land at the local or regional markets. This constitutes a key source of their 'economic accessibility' to acquire healthy and nutritious food.[75] Many debates on subsistence agriculture ignore this aspect. Nowadays, food production for subsistence is only one pillar, albeit an important one, of food security strategies at household level. Third, access to land and natural resources is also entailed in 'physical accessibility'. This holds true for the case if the gathering of fruits, nuts, tubers, fishing and hunting forms a pillar of livelihood and food security strategies. In reality – on the ground – a balanced mix of all three aspects forms the ground of the realization of the right to adequate food and nutrition for most rural communities.

In consequence, the implementation of the right to food means to privilege the right of people who need access to land for food production for exchange or for their own consumption.[76] As the case of Cambodia exemplifies, the opposite happens in this new wave of land grabbing.

6.2. LAND RIGHTS AND HUMAN RIGHTS – A DIFFERENTIATION

In the discussion on legal aspects of land grabs, it is important to recall the nature and difference between human rights and land rights. This is of special importance as discussions on land grabbing quickly mix up those two levels of legal framing. This can be the case when government officials, academics or development practitioners explain that many land grabs are legal. Often the

---

74 It is a bit confusing but access to land is mainly an aspect of availability, rather than accessibility from a human rights perspective. Nevertheless, CESCR General Comment No. 12 also refers to access to land as an aspect of accessibility in the context of ancestral lands of indigenous population groups.

75 CESCR General Comment No. 12: 'Economic accessibility implies that personal or household financial costs associated with the acquisition of food for an adequate diet should be at a level such that the attainment and satisfaction of other basic needs are not threatened or compromised. Economic accessibility applies to any acquisition pattern or entitlement through which people procure their food and is a measure of the extent to which it is satisfactory for the enjoyment of the right to adequate food.'

76 Sometimes human rights language also refers to 'positive action' or 'affirmative action'.

reference frame for this statement is the national statutory land law or even only one of its paragraphs. But this is not spelled out clearly. It is especially not spelled out as a choice for one of multiple legal frames. Such a comment can confuse the debate as an analysis based on the human right to food could reveal that despite a procedural compliance with a specific land regulation basic human rights can have been violated and thus such a land grab can be clearly called illegitimate.

For example, a family might be evicted and it is argued that the national land law does not give them a property right to the land they are evicted from. Quite often the term 'squatters' is used on them to indicate their 'illegality'. But the eviction might still constitute a violation of the human right to food if the family is deprived of its means to feed itself (typically through the loss of access to agricultural land). The human rights lens turns the 'squatter' into a 'rights holder' who has a certain right to the land.

This is why it is important to remember that land rights mostly refer to civil law which gives a regulatory frame for the use and (more and more) ownership rights over land. They are exclusive and non-universal (e.g. 'I have the right to use this specific plot of land'). These land rights typically are discussed between two private persons (legal or natural). This type of rights is mainly used in a defensive manner (e.g. protection from eviction). When human rights, in our case the right to food, come into play, views on conflicts and struggles can be broadened. It can open the perspective from private/individual disputes over land rights to a collective social conflict involving public interest and constitutional principles (e.g. social use of property, equitable access to land). In this sense, the right to food can also be a tool to leave a defensive only approach, as it can challenge existing land rights if they are unjust or discriminatory. It can also challenge international law regimes that work against the poor (e.g. investment treaties).[77] This can expose the fact that at the core of a land conflict is a State failure to implement human rights obligations like protecting and actively providing access to land for landless and land poor people and give back ancestral territories.

The case of Madagascar provides a good example in this regard. In its Concluding Observations, the UN Committee on Economic, Social and Rights, recommended based on the influx of land investments in Madagascar that:

> '... the State party revise Law No. 2007-037 and facilitate the acquisition of land by peasants and persons living in rural areas, as well as their access to natural resources. It also recommends that the State party carry out a national debate on investment in agriculture and seek, prior to any contracts with foreign companies, the free and informed consent of the persons concerned.'[78]

[77] See for example TNI 2014 Licensed to grab. How international investment rules undermine agrarian justice, available at: https://www.tni.org/en/briefing/licensed-grab accessed 27-7-2015).

[78] UN doc. E/C.12/MDG/CO/2, 16 December 2009, CESCR, Forty-third session, Geneva, 2–20 November 2009, p. 4.

Thus, human rights can transform the legal and political framing of a conflict that might be of high relevance for the demands and views of rural social movements. Indeed, today rural social movements already use the right to food as a relevant part of their legal strategies which also support mobilization and forging alliances.

6.3. GLOBAL GOVERNANCE INSTRUMENTS AND THE ISSUE OF DEMOCRATIC LEGITIMACY

Despite the conceptual thoughts and developments highlighted above, a key challenge remains. It is to hold States truly responsible for their human rights obligations. This explicitly includes holding them responsible for their obligation to protect people from human rights abuses by powerful third parties (e.g. powerful persons, companies, funds …). Ideally, States could be held responsible for human rights violations through national and international legal systems. But in practice this is a very complicated task as the international and national justiciability of human rights law is still weak and in many political contexts quite impossible. In this imperfect world we get presented an alternative: a multiverse of governance instruments. Instruments like safeguards, principles and standards that promise some kind of leverage and enforcement of rights.

Based on the de-facto lack of access to justice through public systems people affected by land grabs and NGOs frequently embark on using these instruments. What is not so much done is a critical reflection of the overall nature of these instruments and the context in which they operate. The German legal scholar Goldmann provides an interesting approach to get a more nuanced understanding of these instruments.[79] He uses three sets of parameters to systematically grasp the differences between governance instruments.

- The first are generic parameters. This includes authorship and procedure. It is helpful to indicate the level of legitimacy and authority of an instrument.
- The second are textual parameters. This includes the content, scope and the addressees of an instrument.
- The third are follow-up parameters. In our discussion this includes enforcement mechanisms – from hard (e.g. sanction) to soft (monitor, reporting …).

The experience of FIAN's right to food-based work on land conflict indicates that there is a negative correlation between the legitimacy of these instruments and the systematics and frequency of their application as well as their enforcement

[79] M. Goldmann, 'Inside Relative Normativity: From Sources to Standard Instruments for the Exercise of International Public Authority' (2008) Vol. 9, No. 11 *German Law Journal*, pp. 1865–1908.

mechanisms. Instruments with a very high legitimacy and authority have weak enforcement mechanisms and are applied less systematically. Instruments with less legitimacy are applied more systematically and often have some kind of processual enforcement mechanism. The following examples add some flesh on this observation:

- The Roundtable on Responsible Palm Oil (RSPO) clearly is an instrument driven by companies of the palm oil value chain. One can easily argue that the legitimacy of this instrument is very low. In addition regarding the addressee, the instrument starts from a company perspective and is not rooted in international human rights law. Nevertheless, RSPO standards are applied broadly (following their website 20% of the global palm oil production)[80] and they have an internal dispute settlement facility.[81]
- A second example is the World Bank safeguards. These safeguard set out a range of basic criteria that selected World Bank activities must meet. Their elaboration is controlled by a few powerful States (the G7 countries alone hold almost half of the votes).[82] International human rights law does not play a role. The inspection panel is the place where complaints can be addressed to try to enforce these safeguards. These safeguards are not only applied in the Bank's own projects but many bilateral development banks employ them thus making them one of the most used governance instruments in development politics globally.

Both instruments – World Bank safeguards and RSPO – are very good in creating the illusion that some basic globally accepted rules and accountability mechanisms are in place. In view of the fact that they are elaborated and controlled by a few powerful States and/or companies these instruments are profoundly illegitimate.

An example on the other end of the spectrum is the UN Land Tenure Guidelines (TGs). Based on regional and stakeholder consultations, they have been extensively negotiated by the Committee on World Food Security (CFS) systematically involving the States and civil society.[83] They are strongly rooted in existing human rights law and were adopted by the CFS through consensus. The CFS, as a global governance body, has been mandated with this task, so they have an extremely high legitimacy. On the other hand, three years after their adoption, implementation is still rather punctuated and limited resources are made available to implement them. They also have a soft follow-up mechanism:

---

80 See www.rspo.org/about, accessed 27-7-2015.

81 On the critique of this internal mechanism see for example http://wrm.org.uy/articles-from-the-wrm-bulletin/section1/indonesia-how-rspo-addressed-concerns-raised-against-first-resources-one-of-its-members/, accessed 27-7-2015.

82 A safeguard review process is actually ongoing.

83 See section 1 of this chapter on the CFS Civil Society Mechanism.

their implementation should be monitored at the CFS. And even this mechanism is much contested.

In today's context, where power relations are by far more decisive than human rights, people's mobilization remains the paramount form of human rights accountability. In this regard, governance instruments should not only be assessed based on their legitimacy but also based on their power to support or distract from mobilization.

In the meantime, some more legitimate governance instruments, like the UN Land Tenure Guidelines, can effectively be strengthened when social movements, supported by NGOs, claim, monitor and implement them themselves. In addition, we need to make human rights treaties and human rights law, especially the human right to food and related rights to land and water truly enforceable. FIAN tries to tackle this challenge in multiple ways. Apart from concrete case work, where we try to support people when their right to food is violated, we support the enhancement of the international human rights system.

- We supported the elaboration and adoption of the Optional Protocol (OP) to the International Covenant on Economic, Social and Cultural Rights. Through the OP the Committee on Economic, Social and Cultural Rights has the competence to receive complaints related to the rights enshrined in the Covenant – including the right to food. Now we advocate for the ratification of the OP by the States.[84]
- We try to expand the understanding and systematic application of extraterritorial human rights obligations (ETOs). This means that States are to be held accountable for human rights obligations also outside their territories when this is within their sphere of influence (e.g. when the State is active outside its boundaries or when it is in a position to regulate a company). The Maastricht Principles on Extraterritorial Obligation of States in the area of Economic, Social and Cultural Rights, finalized in 2012 are the normative basis for this work.[85]
- We support the work towards a binding treaty to regulate human rights abuses of transnational corporations (TNCs). In 2014 a global call for such a binding instrument was supported by more than 600 CSOs. This call was taken up by the Human Rights Council in 2014. An intergovernmental working group at the Human Rights Council started working on this issue.
- We support the process towards a United Nations declaration on the rights of peasants and other people working in rural areas that is led by the global peasant network La Via Campesina. The draft declaration includes a right to land as the very basis for a peasants' self-determined life in dignity and social

[84] In April 2016, 21 States had ratified the OP.
[85] See www.etoconsortium.org/en/library/maastricht-principles/.

reproduction. This also brings us to the final sub-section of this chapter, the emerging discussion on a human right to land.

6.4. A HUMAN RIGHT TO LAND

Back in 1990 the Special Rapporteur on the Realization of Economic, Social and Cultural Rights, Danilo Türk, emphasized:

> 'The fulfilment of various economic, social and cultural rights show a direct relationship to land, such as the right to food, the right to housing, the right to an adequate standard of living, the right to culture, the rights of indigenous peoples and others.
>
> The Special Rapporteur is fully aware of the delicate nature and controversy surrounding issues relating to land issues internationally, yet feels convinced that the time has come to give this fundamental issue the serious attention it deserves. No question is more central to power relations within society or to issues of equality and income distribution than land.'[86]

Indeed, there is a normative and legal basis that exists around which to operationalize the human right to land. International human rights law already recognizes the right to land for indigenous and tribal peoples in ILO Convention 169 and the UN Declaration on the Rights of Indigenous Peoples (UNDRIP). Also important, 25 years after Danilo Türk's report, international human rights advocacy and practice have more and more recognized that for all human beings and communities land is indispensable for the enjoyment of various economic, social, and cultural rights, such as the right to food, the right to housing, the right to an adequate standard of living, the right to culture, the right to work, and the right to self-determination, and for rural women's rights.[87]

---

86 UN doc. E/CN.4/Sub.2/1990/19, 6 July 1990, Commission on Human Rights, *The new international economic order and the promotion of human rights; Realization of Economic. Social and Cultural Rights*, Progress report prepared by Mr. Danilo Türk.

87 UN doc. A/64/170, 23 July 2009, *Seed policies and the right to food: enhancing agrobiodiversity and encouraging innovation*, Report by the Special Rapporteur on the right to food Olivier de Schutter; O, de Schutter, 'The emerging human right to land', (2010) Vol. 12(3) *International Community Law Review*, pp. 303–334; UN doc. A/65/281, 11 August 2010, Interim Report of the Special Rapporteur on the Right to Food, Olivier de Schutter; T. Gelbspan, V. Nagaraj '*Seeding hope? Land in the international human rights agenda: challenges and prospects*' (2012) (ESCR Net and International Council on Human Rights Policy); UN doc. A/HRC/4/18, 5 February 2007, Report of the Special Rapporteur on adequate housing as a component of the right to an adequate standard of living, Miloon Kothari; OHCHR, 2010, Consultation on Land and Human Rights: Background paper prepared by the Research and Right to Development Division (RRDD), Human Rights and Economic and Social Issues Section (HRESIS).

In the context of (1) ongoing violations of all these rights, (2) the complexity in which land grabbing takes place and (3) the myriad of segmented interest-driven 'answers', Künnemann and Monsalve pose the following question:

> 'What would be a more expansive concept around which to build global governance that addresses the full set of challenges posed by the current wave of land grabbing and the increasing interference by international actors and policies in local enjoyment of land?'[88]

The answer lies in an operationalisation of the human right to land. Taking the human rights listed above as a starting point and practicing the 'indivisibility, interdependency and interrelatedness' of these rights,[89] the following framing for a human right to land has been put forward:

> 'This is the right – individually and in community with others – to effectively access, use and control land and related natural resources in order to feed and house themselves, and to live and develop their cultures and territories partly in a self-determined way where appropriate. It is a right that is limited to the use of land by communities and individuals for reproduction and commercial purposes. It is different from the right to private property, and does not primarily refer to the right to buy and sell land. The human right to land entails a geographic dimension that privileges the local, and does not condone control of faraway lands by absentee owners.'[90]

This framing resonates with the demands of social movements. It opposes the fragmentation of their lives (e.g. land as economic asset) and it is embedded in a call for a democratic land control. Coming back to the historic starting point, the struggle for human rights has always been one of decades and centuries. These struggles have always started with the recognition for rights. 'The contemporary struggles around a human right to land are part of this evolving history.'[91]

---

[88] Künnemann, 2013, p. 129.
[89] See for example the Vienna Declaration and Programme of Action 1993, Article I.5.
[90] Borras *et al*, 2015, p. 611.
[91] Künnemann, 2013, p. 136.

WOMEN'S RIGHT TO LAND: A COMPARISON BETWEEN INTERNATIONAL LEGAL OBLIGATIONS AND CUSTOMARY LAWS IN BALI (INDONESIA) AND IN ACHOLI (UGANDA)

Ingrid Westendorp and Elin Hilwig

1. INTRODUCTION

Because of its connection to several basic human rights, land can be regarded as the most important property a human being can possess. There is an obvious link to food, housing, and employment, but autonomy and decision-making powers may be connected to land as well. Possession of land can secure a person's position in society and may open doors to a better life because it can serve as collateral for credits and loans. Land can also be the collective property of a group or community thus determining this group's identity and asserting its claim to land that has been in their possession for several generations. All over the world, it is more difficult for women than for men to obtain property rights over land although a large part of the agrarian workers is female.[1]

This situation clashes with the principles of equality and non-discrimination that have been acknowledged by the great majority of the States in the world when they became parties to human rights treaties, particularly the Convention on the Elimination of Discrimination Against Women (hereafter the Women's Convention). States Parties that wish to accommodate ethnic and religious groups by according them special personal rights usually create a very difficult situation for the women belonging to such groups since traditional customary

1 'Women comprise, on average, 43 percent of the agricultural labour force in developing countries, ranging from 20 percent in Latin America to 50 percent in Eastern Asia and sub-Saharan Africa': FAO (Food and Agriculture Organization of the United Nations) 'The State of food and agriculture 2010–2011 – Women in Agriculture – closing the gender gap, www.fao.org/docrep/013/i2050e00.htm, accessed 04-02-2016.

beliefs that form the core of personal laws are generally not easily paired to the concept of equality. As a result, women, including female farmers, may never have an autonomous right to land. This does not mean, however, that traditional practices and customary laws regarding land are always negative for women.

The premise of this paper is that tradition and customary rules need to be closely examined in light of women's right to land in the context of a State's human rights obligations, particularly the obligation to achieve equality between the sexes both in law and in practice. When custom has a negative effect on women's land rights, it needs to be modified or abolished. However, traditional rules that work to women's advantage should be maintained. The question is who is best suited to assess and if necessary modify customary rules and traditions and which measures should be taken to bring about such a change? An important worry in this regard is that change is brought about in such a way that it is acceptable to the population and that it will leave a group's unique cultural identity unaffected.

In this paper we compare women's property rights of land in two areas of the world where land rights are mainly governed by customary law and tradition; in Bali (Indonesia) and in Acholi (Uganda). By customary law we understand the rules that are generally accepted as binding and authoritative among individuals belonging to a certain group or community.

The terms property and property rights are used in a very broad sense here. They range from mere access rights to easements, sharecropping, usufruct, rental, leasing, and ultimately ownership over land. For an individual or group of individuals the most important aspect of these various forms of both informal and formal property rights will be that they enjoy security of tenure: active security denoting the ability to perform transactions concerning the piece of land and passive security guaranteeing that they will not run the risk of being evicted from their land.[2]

The case of Bali is especially interesting because while women's land rights are under discussion in many developing countries and some progress has been made, in Bali the situation paradoxically seems to have gone backward rather than forward since the fall of Suharto in 1998. The change in regime was the start of far-reaching decentralisation and autonomy for various regions in Indonesia, among which Bali. The local authorities used their powers to fall back on and maintain traditions and customary rules to strengthen the Balinese cultural identity and distinguish it from other parts of Indonesia.[3] With respect to land rights, Balinese tradition and customs work to women's detriment. They put the

2 *Handling Land: Innovative tools for land governance and secure tenure*, United Nations Human Settlements Programme (UN-Habitat), Nairobi, 2012, p. 24.

3 CEDAW/C/IDN/CO/5, Concluding Observations Indonesia, 2007, para. 12.

women belonging to the Hindu population – the great majority of whom want to belong to the group and respect the traditions – in a very tight spot. These women have little choice but foregoing human rights they are entitled to. If they insist in claiming their rights, they run the risk of being accused of undermining the group's cultural identity and they may be ostracized by their family and community. In addition, customs and traditions have become static and inflexible because the group has an interest to uphold rules that are different from the mainstream to identify itself.[4]

The land rights situation in Acholi can be placed in a very different context. Some of the main challenges with regard to the land rights of Acholi women, have their roots in the recent history of insurgency and armed hostility in Northern Uganda. Acholi was the centre of the (1986–2006) conflict between the Lord's Resistance Army (LRA) and the Central Government, which caused as much as 90 percent of the population of Acholi Sub-Region to become internally displaced.[5] Typically, when people become displaced due to conflict, land conflicts arise upon return. The types of problems that arise are, for instance, that early returnees have confiscated property or that late returnees are unsure about the boundaries after many years of absence. Many people who knew where the boundaries were have died in the conflict or through the elapse of time. Another major issue around conflict and displacement is the issue of demoralisation of society. Through social breakdown the clan's ability to enforce its traditional rules of protection are weakened.[6]

Apart from these remnants of conflict, northern Uganda is further affected by misgovernment, corruption and marginalisation by the Central Government. While the end of armed hostilities has opened up economic opportunities, the very fact that Northern Uganda is rich in resources (oil, gold, timber, and the agricultural potential of the soil) puts the people who live there into a precarious

4 A. Shachar, *Multicultural Jurisdictions; Cultural Differences and Women's Rights*, Cambridge University Press, Cambridge 2001, pp. 39 and 84–85.

5 C. Dolan, 'Uganda Strategic Conflict Analysis' 2006 *Sida*, www.sida.se/Publications/Import/pdf/sv/Uganda-Strategic-Conflict-Analysis_376.pdf accessed 04-02-2016, p. 12. At the conflicts peak in 2005 there were nearly 1.84 million people in 251 IDP camps across 11 districts of northern Uganda: 'UNHCR closes chapter on Uganda's internally displaced people – Briefing Notes, 6 January 2012' *UNHCR* www.unhcr.org/4f06e2a79.html accessed 04-02-2016.

6 Specifically regarding Northern Uganda, where the Acholi Sub-Region is situated, see: M.A. Rugadya, 'Associates Research Occasional Paper No. 4 – Unveiling gender, Land and Property rights in Post-Conflict Northern Uganda' 2008 http://citeseerx.ist.psu.edu/viewdoc/download?doi=10.1.1.431.5246&rep=rep1&type=pdf, accessed 04-02-2016, p. 7.

position.[7] However, Acholi still has land in abundance and the sub-region under scrutiny consists predominantly of rural areas.

The research methodology we used for this paper consists of a review of relevant UN instruments and documents, national and local legislation and traditions, a literature search, as well as field research. The field research in Bali and Acholi constituted of conducting interviews with the help of prepared questions.[8] Both in Bali and in Acholi representatives of NGOs have been interviewed as well as academics. In Bali the field research also included interviewing provincial authorities and men and women living in urban and rural areas between the ages of 17 and 75.[9]

In the following, section 2 will go into the international human rights framework that is relevant to women's land rights. Subsequently, Indonesia's international and national legal framework will be discussed in section 3, while the specific situation in Bali is examined in section 4. Along similar lines, the existing framework in Uganda, and the particular situation in Acholi will be under scrutiny in sections 5 and 6 respectively. Section 7 gives an analysis of the two cases by indicating the differences and the similarities and outlining possible solutions to further women's land rights in both regions. Finally, some concluding remarks will be made in section 8.

2. THE INTERNATIONAL HUMAN RIGHTS FRAMEWORK RELEVANT TO WOMEN'S LAND RIGHTS

At the international level, three human rights conventions are the most relevant in the context of women's equal right to land. The International Covenant on Economic, Social, and Cultural Rights (ICESCR), the International Covenant on Civil and Political Rights (ICCPR) – both adopted by the UN General Assembly in 1966 – and the Women's Convention, adopted in 1979. States that become parties to these treaties take legal obligations upon themselves, not just at the central level, but also at the regional and local level, irrespective of any national

---

7 M. Llamazares, 'Northern Uganda Conflict analysis report' *ACCS (Advisory Consortium on Conflict Sensitivity)* 2013, www.saferworld.org.uk/resources/view-resource/762-northern-uganda-conflict-analysis accessed 04-02-2016, pp. 10–11.

8 The research in Bali was conducted by Ingrid Westendorp while the research in Acholi was done by Elin Hilwig. The authors conducted their research quite independently from each other in 2012 and 2013 respectively, but decided to combine their findings in this paper.

9 A list with the names of all the interviewees both in Acholi and in Bali is in the possession of the authors.

arrangements that have been made such as regional autonomy,[10] or a personal law system for an ethnic or religious group.[11]

Like all human rights instruments, these treaties are based on the principle of equality between the sexes and the prohibition of discrimination on the basis of sex.[12] The monitoring bodies of the three conventions, the Committee on the Elimination of Discrimination Against Women (CEDAW), the Committee on Economic, Social, and Cultural Rights (CESCR), and the Human Rights Committee (HRC) respectively, all have further clarified and interpreted the meaning of these principles in General Recommendations (GRs) – also General Comments (GCs) – that are to be considered as authoritative interpretations of provisions of the Conventions.[13]

In the past, discrimination against women was understood as discrimination based on sex – i.e. treating a woman less favourably because of her biological – specifically reproductive – characteristics. Nowadays, also discrimination based on gender is taken into account. This entails that it is acknowledged that discrimination against women may also be founded on culturally determined roles, stereotypes, and prejudices that have a negative bearing on women's socio-economic positions.[14] In many societies, the stereotypical roles women are expected to play are seen as complementary, but inferior to men's.

Gendered ideas also have an impact on men's choices in life. Men are supposed to be decision-makers and breadwinners who bear the financial responsibility for their families. While this limits men's choices in life, it also means that in many parts of the world boys and men receive preferential treatment in the family

---

10 M. Shaw, *International Law*, Cambridge University Press, Cambridge 2014, p. 161. The Human Rights Committee (HRC) puts it as follows: 'The obligations of the Covenant [...] are binding on every State Party as a whole. All branches of government (executive, legislative and judicial), and other public or governmental authorities, at whatever level – national, regional or local – are in a position to engage the responsibility of the State Party'. Human Rights Committee, General Comment (GC) No 31, the nature of the general legal obligations imposed on States Parties to the Covenant, 26-05-2004, para. 4.

11 A personal law system entails that family law rules like marriage, divorce, legal capacity and guardianship, maintenance, inheritance, intestacy and succession, are determined by an ethnic or religious group independently from the national legislator and will apply to anyone belonging to such a group.

12 The principles of equality and non-discrimination may be found in ICESCR Articles 2 and 3; ICCPR Articles 2, 3, and 26; Women's Convention Articles 1, 2, 3 and 5.

13 Of particular importance in the context of this paper are HRC GC No 28, Equality of rights between men and women (Article 3), 29 March 2000; CESCR GC No 16, Article 3: the equal right of men and women to the enjoyment of all economic, social and cultural rights, 13 May 2005; CEDAW General Recommendation (GR) No 28, on the core obligations of States parties under Article 2 of the Convention, 16 December 2010.

14 CEDAW defines gender as: 'socially constructed identities, attributes and roles for women and men and society's social and cultural meaning for these biological differences resulting in hierarchical relationships between women and men and in the distribution of power and rights favouring men and disadvantaging women'. CEDAW GR No 28, para. 5.

particularly in respect to their education and the inheritance. When gender is taken into account, the root causes of discrimination against women come to the surface and can be tackled. This is exactly the intention of Article 5(a) of the Women's Convention: it is not enough when State Parties adopt laws that prohibit discrimination: they should also take 'all appropriate measures' to modify the harmful patterns that are based on stereotypes and prejudices that form the basis for the systemic discrimination against women in practice.

It is not just CEDAW whose approach of discrimination against women has changed. Also the HRC and the CESCR have interpreted the prohibition of discrimination based on sex in Article 3 of their respective conventions as including the concept of gender.[15] The HRC is the more explicit of the two by stating in GC No 28 that States parties are obliged to ensure that attitudes that are rooted in culture, religion and tradition are not to be used as justifications to maintain inequality between men and women.[16] Furthermore, it is pertinent that this Committee has also declared that the protection of minority rights in Article 27 of the ICCPR finds it boundaries where women's right to equality is threatened.[17]

As far as the right to equality is concerned, the three Committees agree that it should not only exist in law as formal or *de iure* equality, but it should also be enjoyed in practice. That is why *de facto* or substantive equality should be achieved as well.[18] Formal equality should not only be realized by abolishing all laws and regulations that discriminate against women – including such laws that have been adopted at regional or local level – but also entails that new laws are adopted that promote equality between women and men.[19] Furthermore, legislative bodies should see to it that seemingly neutral laws and policies do not have a negative impact on women's rights in practice.[20] This may require that measures are taken to prevent, modify, or abolish attitudes that cause or support existing *de facto* inequality. States parties' obligations thus comprise equal treatment, equal opportunities *and* equal results for women if compared to men. The latter implies that it is sometimes allowed or necessary to treat women and men unequally – particularly treat women more favourably – in order to achieve an equal result.[21]

---

15 HRC GC No 28, paras 5–7 and CESCR GC No 16, paras 5–8, 11 and 18.

16 HRC GC No 28, para. 5.

17 HCR GC 28, para. 32.

18 CEDAW GR No 25, para 4 and paras 8 and 9; HRC GC No 28, para 3; CESCR GC No 20, para 8.

19 CESCR GC No 16, para. 18.

20 CEDAW GR No 29, para. 8.

21 Article 4(1) of the Women's Convention allows, and sometimes demands, temporary special measures in order to accelerate equality between men and women; such measures should not be regarded as discriminatory against men and have to stop when a certain goal has been achieved. CEDAW GR No 25, para. 24.

Women's equal right to property should not be affected by a change in their civil status.[22] Married women have equal rights to own, acquire, manage, enjoy and dispose of property and there are no justifications to apply discriminatory laws or customs on women. Marital property that was accumulated during the marriage should be divided equally over husband and wife upon the dissolution of the marriage.[23]

As regards inheritance law, States parties are under an obligation to repeal all laws and modify any customs that discriminate between men and women in this respect, and they have to ensure that women and men who are in the same degree of relationship with the deceased will receive an equal share.[24] Personal status laws that discriminate against women in relation to marriage, divorce, inheritance or other family law matters are held to be in violation of Articles 2, 5, 15, and 16 of the Women's Convention and should be abolished.

In spite of the international rights and obligations discussed above, generally speaking women have fewer land rights and less control over land than men, which may consequently affect the realization of other human rights, especially in respect of their living conditions.[25] In the next few sections the legal frameworks of Indonesia and Uganda will be under scrutiny with a view to determining to what extent these States have committed themselves to international standards and how this commitment has been translated into national law and practice.

3. INDONESIA – INTERNATIONAL AND NATIONAL LEGAL FRAMEWORK

3.1. INTRODUCTION

For 350 years Indonesia was a Dutch colony. The Dutch introduced their civil law system – which is still largely in place – but they respected the customary rules, called Adat law, as far as personal laws of groups and communities were concerned. Dutch lawyers started to meticulously codify existing Adat rules and until today a comprehensive collection of written Adat law can be found at the Van Vollenhoven Instituut in Leiden, the Netherlands.

On 17 August 1945, Indonesia declared its independence and shortly afterwards the Constitution was adopted. After the war of independence with the Netherlands that lasted till 1949, the country was firmly ruled from Jakarta, first by the authoritarian regime of President Sukarno, followed by three decades

22 CEDAW GRs No 21 and No 29; HRC GCs No 19 and No 28; CESCR GCs No 16 and No 20.
23 CEDAW GR No 21, para. 32, and GR No 29, paras 43–48.
24 CEDAW GR No 29, paras 49–53; HRC GC No 28, para. 26; CESCR GC No 16, para. 27.
25 FAO, IFAD and ILC, *Rural Women's Access to Land and Property in Selected Countries*, 2004, p. 10.

of the 'New Order Regime' of President Suharto. The fall of Suharto in 1998 and the subsequent reformation (*Reformasi*) brought two changes that are relevant here: a commitment to international human rights law and decentralization. In this section, first Indonesia's international human rights obligations will be under scrutiny, followed by an assessment of the implementation of these obligations in the national legal framework. The last part will deal with the issue of decentralization.

3.2. INTERNATIONAL LEGAL FRAMEWORK

Indonesia became a party to the Women's Convention in 1984 and to the ICESCR and the ICCPR in 2006. Since no relevant reservations were made, the provisions on non-discrimination and equality fully apply in respect of the obligations of the State and all its organs, including those at the central, provincial, and local level.

In order to further women's equality Indonesia has created a State Ministry for the Empowerment of Women and Child Protection that coordinates efforts to enhance women's position in society, tries to raise awareness of the Women's Convention, and seeks to educate Government officials.[26] Until now it seems that these efforts have had a limited impact since in-depth knowledge about the human rights contained in the Convention and the State's corollary obligations is not widely spread. As extensive dissemination among the population is also lacking, many women are neither aware of their rights under the Conventions nor know how to claim them.[27]

A complicating factor with regard to the implementation of international law is that it is unclear whether Indonesia has a monist or a dualist system in respect of the relationship between international treaty obligations and domestic law.[28] The consequence is that if local authorities and courts understand the system as dualistic they may only take national laws into account instead of directly applying the human rights treaties that Indonesia is a party to. The Constitution does not contain a provision clarifying this matter and much confusion exists because of inconsistencies in respect of the implementation of international treaties. While some scholars think that international rights can only be enjoyed when they have been transposed into national law, the Human Rights Act No. 39 of 1999 seems to propagate monism in Article 7 by determining that everyone

---

26 CEDAW/C/IDN/6-7, Combined sixth and seventh periodic reports Indonesia, 7 January 2011, para. 2.

27 CEDAW/C/IDN/6-7, 2011, para. 1; CCPR/C/IDN/CO/1, Concluding Observations of the Human Rights Committee on Indonesia's initial report, 21 August 2013, para. 5.

28 Monists have a unitary view of law: international and national law form one system in which international law takes precedence over national law. Dualists understand international and national law as two separate systems. International law rules must be converted into national law before they can be applied in a court of law. Shaw, 2014, pp. 93–95.

can use both national and international human rights law – to the extent that treaties have been ratified by Indonesia – when his or her rights are violated.[29] Article 67 of the same Act states that everyone has to comply with international law ratified by Indonesia implying that it is prohibited for local authorities to ignore international obligations or to give precedence to local law.

3.3. NATIONAL LEGAL FRAMEWORK

3.3.1. Constitution

The Constitution of the Republic of Indonesian (Constitution) was adopted in 1945 and has meanwhile been amended four times.[30] The principles of non-discrimination and equality are included in Articles 27(1) and 28 I(2) of the Constitution, but there is no specific provision dealing with discrimination against women.

3.3.2. Human Rights Act

Though the Human Rights Act (HRA) is the instrument that is particularly used to include human rights and connected obligations, not all human rights obligations are contained in it. In Article 3, equality and non-discrimination is propagated, while (married) women's equal right to property is guaranteed by Articles 36 and 51. Article 45 states that women's rights are human rights, but a few crucial provisions of the Women's Convention are absent; a clear definition of discrimination based on sex is lacking as well as an obligation to modify stereotypes and harmful traditional practices in line with Article 5. The latter is the more so a pity since the Indonesian Government acknowledges that modifying existing stereotypes and gender specific roles in society remains one of the major challenges in respect of the implementation of the Women's Convention.[31] Certain efforts are undertaken to change people's mind sets, particularly stereotyped ideas that are impelled by old religious rules. For instance, school books and curricula were reviewed and media campaigns were held, but it seems that these efforts are especially focused on the Muslim population and traditional Islamic teachings.[32] In the reports that were submitted to CEDAW, no mention is made of attempts

[29] Aryo Dewanto Wisnu, 'Implementing Treaties in Municipal Courts', in: *Mimbar Hukum* (Quarterly Journal Faculty of Law Universitas Gadjah Mada), Vol. 23, No. 1, February 2011, pp. 235–236.

[30] The 1945 Constitution of the Republic of Indonesia (*Undang-Undang Dasar*, 1945), currently the Fourth Amendment of 2002 is being used.

[31] CEDAW/C/IDN/4-5, Combined fourth and fifth periodic reports Indonesia, 27 July 2005, paras 52–59.

[32] CEDAW/C/IDN/6-7, 2011, paras 32–36.

to modify discriminatory Hindu customs or stereotypes that undermine Hindu women's right to equality.

3.3.3. *Basic Agrarian Law*

The Basic Agrarian Law No 5/1960 (BAL) is the most important law in respect to all matters that concern land. Article 9 of the BAL awards equality to men and women as far as property rights over land are concerned, but the approach is formal; every person who has enough financial means is allowed to buy land. Though it is important that there are no legal barriers that prevent women from having property rights over land, such an approach does not take the different socio-economic positions of men and women into account and thus does not contribute to the achievement of equality of result. Indonesia is basically an agrarian State and about half of the Indonesian population – and thus half of Indonesian women – lives in rural areas.[33] Access to and property rights of land are therefore of the utmost importance. However, by and large, titles of ownership over land will be put in the name of male head of the family.[34]

3.3.4. *Marriage Act*

Article 1 of the Marriage Act No 1/1974 (MA) acknowledges that husband and wife are equal and have equal rights. Property acquired during marriage, including land and housing, is regarded as marriage community and consequently both spouses have equal rights to administer it and both are entitled to half of this joint property in case of divorce. However, the object and purpose of Article 5 of the Women's Convention is encroached upon by the statement in Article 31(3) of the MA that the husband is to be regarded as the head of the household, while the wife is responsible for the household and raising the children.[35]

---

[33] According to the latest count, 54% of the Indonesian population lives in urban areas. The pull of the cities is very strong. In comparison; in 2005, 46% of the population lived in the city. See www.worldometers.info/world-population/indonesia-population, consulted on 20 May 2015.

[34] Koalisi Perempuan Indonesia Untuk Keadilan dan Demokrasi (*Indonesian Women's Coalition for Justice and Democracy*), Implementation of the Convention on the Elimination of All Forms of Discrimination against Women in Indonesia, Fulfilment of the Rights of Rural Women Article 14, Jakarta, May 2012, para. 12. For their report the NGO conducted research in 147 villages in 45 Districts in 10 Provinces from April 2011 to May 2012. This included research in Bali, in particular in the districts/city Tabanan, Karangasem and Denpasar.

[35] Also see CEDAW/C/IDN/4-5, 2005, para. 161 and CEDAW/C/IDN/6-7, 2011, para. 35. While some changes have happened in the six years between the two reports, the traditional division of power, work, and responsibilities within the family has remained the same.

3.4. DECENTRALIZATION

The decentralization began in 1999 when Law No 22 on Local Government was adopted which gave provincial, district, and municipal governments more autonomy and control over the budget. Regional autonomy was further laid down in Articles 18–18B of the Constitution and lastly updated in Law No. 32/2004 on Local Government. For women, one of the consequences of the decentralization has been that the realization of their rights, including land rights, is now more than before in the hands of the provincial and local authorities. According to CEDAW, in many instances this development has had an adverse effect on the realization of women's rights.[36] Indonesia confirmed this by stating that many regional laws are discriminatory and in contravention of national law.[37]

In spite of the decentralization and irrespective of the constitutional arrangements that have been made, under international law ultimately the State will remain responsible for all actions by State organs, also subordinate or local organs. In cases where local legislation is in violation with international obligations, the central Government has the duty to persuade the local authorities to amend this situation, while the local authorities for their part are obliged to meet the international obligations that the State has taken upon itself.[38] This is also true for human rights obligations.[39] Indonesia has accepted the responsibility for all governmental actions in Article 28 I(4) of the Constitution and in Article 8 of the HRA.

4. SITUATION IN BALI

4.1. BACKGROUND

Hindu tradition, which originates from the *Manawa Dharmasastra* (the Hindu holy book) that had an important influence on Balinese Adat law, is based on the idea that men and women are inherently of equal worth. However, because they are supposed to play different roles in society, they do not have to the same rights but they are entitled to different privileges that are commensurate with their societal roles. In line with this thinking, the Adat rules in respect to family, marriage, and inheritance are not based on equality between men and women, but on *equity*; a person will have rights and duties that befit their gender and

36 CEDAW/C/IDN/CO/5, Concluding Comments Indonesia, 10 August 2007, para. 12.

37 CEDAW/C/IDN/6-7, 2011, para. 23.

38 SHAW, 2014, p. 161.

39 CCPR/C/IDN/CO/1, HRC Concluding Observations on Indonesia's initial report, 2013, paras 5–6, as well as CEDAW/C/IDN/CO/6-7, CEDAW Concluding Observations on Indonesia's sixth and seventh report, 2012, paras 15–16.

status in society.[40] In practice, this comes down to son-preference because a son will remain in the family and he bears the most important responsibilities in respect of religious ceremonies including cremation rites, the most significant ones because of the belief in reincarnation.[41] Based on the custom of female exogamy, a woman who marries leaves her own blood relatives. She supposedly no longer has responsibilities towards her own family because she becomes part of the family of her husband who will take care of her. That is why it is considered wasteful to leave part of the most valuable family assets to a daughter. In fact, married women are treated the same as men who have deliberately abandoned their parental family and the family's responsibilities.[42] Since a son is destined to be a breadwinner, he needs property and money to take care of the financial responsibility for his family and to carry out the family's responsibilities towards the community and the temples.

4.2. BALINESE ADAT LAW AND TRADITION ON LAND

Due to tourism, land has become very expensive in Bali. For the great majority of people it is impossible to save enough money to buy land and the most common manner in which property rights are gained over land is by way of inheritance. However, the Balinese Adat law on inheritance is patrilineal with in principle no inheritance rights for girls and women. The law on inheritance was codified by the then Commissioner (*Residen*) of Bali and Lombok, Frederik Liefrinck in Regulation (*Peswara*) 13 October 1900, particularly Articles 2 and 3. Women, especially widows, play a very minor role in it. They are not regarded as autonomous persons, but as people who have to be taken care of. The estate will go to the son(s) who will provide for the mother.

A daughter has no right to inherit from her father because the heavy responsibilities in relation to religious ceremonies, the forebears, other members of the Hindu community, the temples, land and housing, have to be shouldered by her brother(s). While girls and women also have responsibilities – and quite extensive ones – these are largely ignored or regarded as less important. Unmarried daughters are entitled to the enjoyment of their parents' property and parents may decide to give certain assets to their daughters while they are alive, but the gifts to the daughter(s) have to be relatively modest since the inheritance of the son(s) should not be endangered.[43]

---

40 Equity appears to be positive for women since it is synonymous to fairness, but it is especially used to distribute assets unequally between men and women in correspondence to unequally valued responsibilities. H. Charlesworth, C. Chinkin, *The Boundaries of International Law; A Feminist Analysis*, Manchester University Press, Manchester 2000, p. 80.

41 M. Covarrubias, *Island of Bali*, Periplus Editions, Singapore 1973, pp. 337–338.

42 W. Windia, *Tanya Jawab Hukum Adat Bali* (Questions and Answers on Balinese Customary Law), Majelis Utama Desa Pakrman Bali, Denpasar 2010, p. 136.

43 Windia, 2010, p.146.

Because of the custom of female exogamy, married women will mostly live in the house and on the land that belongs to the husband's family. Consequently, a widow does not inherit from her husband but the estate will be passed on to his sons, and in their absence, to his nephews or other male relatives. This means that for access to housing and land, a widow depends either on her son(s) or on her in-laws. When she has a son, mostly there will not be a problem and she will enjoy this privilege for the rest of her life.[44] Problems arise if the in-laws want to use the land and housing for themselves or if the widow does not behave in accordance with societal rules, implying that she is involved in a romantic relationship with a man. While a widow is in principle allowed to remarry, having an affair is considered a *faux pas* and a reason to evict her from the home and land. In such a case, most women will also be ostracized by their blood relatives.[45] When a widow remarries, she will move to the home of her new husband.

The fact that women are dependent on a man for land and housing also has consequences for women who are involved in an abusive relationship. According to local NGOs, domestic violence is a huge problem and the primary reason why women file for divorce.[46] If women are not economically independent, the consequence may be, however, that they become destitute. In line with Art 1 Marriage Act, the Adat law was changed in 2010 by the *Majelis Utama Desa Pakraman Bali* (MUDP) (Supreme Assembly of the Village Council) with the adoption of a Decree stipulating that during *biasa* (normal) marriage, husband and wife have the same status and property rights in relation to the marital community which consists of property that has been acquired during the marriage. Upon divorce, a woman is entitled to half of the marriage community.[47] However, since the Decree has not yet been converted into a provincial law (*Adat Perda Bali*), and its contents have not been widely disseminated or socially accepted, women who relied on this new rule and who filed for divorce were not awarded their share by the District Courts.[48]

If her parents are still alive, a divorcee who cannot sustain herself can return to her parental home with the status of an unmarried girl which entails that she will resume her obligations towards her own family and will enjoy the same

---

44 Two widows in Karangasem, 55 and 75 years old, related about similar experiences; they could remain in the house belonging to their late husband's family because one of their sons came to live with them. Interviews on 27 and 28 October 2012.

45 This issue was raised by several women, but especially by a 56-year-old female lecturer in Adat law explaining that the rules are very strict. Though the sanction is harsh, i.e. homelessness, this can easily be avoided by a widow by 'behaving' herself. Denpasar, 11 October 2012.

46 Interviews with representatives of KIAS, Komunitas untuk Indonesia yang Adil dan Setara (*Indonesian Society for Honesty and Equality*) and the Indonesian Legal Aid Foundation (ILAF) in Denpasar, 24-10-2012.

47 Decree No 01/Kep/Psm-3/MDP Bali/X/2010, Majelis Utama Desa Pakraman Bali, Denpasar, 15th October 2010. This concerns the property acquired during the marriage.

48 Interviews with representatives of KIAS and ILAF on 24 October 2012.

privileges that she had before marriage.[49] In many cases, mothers will fear that they will lose their children if they file for divorce, since according to Adat law, children born in wedlock will belong to their father's family and courts will assign them to the father, unless they are still very small.[50] Even if a mother gets custody over her child, it may be hard for her to maintain the child in view of her limited financial means and in many cases inadequate housing conditions.[51]

Category of person	Access to their blood relatives' land	Access to their husband's family's land
Unmarried woman	•	
Married woman		•
Widow		•
Divorced woman	•	

Access to land of Balinese women according to Balinese Adat law.

The existing inequality in the law is defended by the Provincial authorities who claim that they do not have to implement Indonesian national laws because of Bali's autonomy and the respect that is due for the Hindu personal status. The fact that international obligations also call for measures at the provincial level as regards law-making, the judiciary and public policy is not understood. Instead, local authorities seem convinced that such obligations are not their concern.[52]

Although much has changed in the course of time, the traditional ideas about men and women for the greater part have persevered and continue to prevent girls and women from inheriting land and housing from fathers and husbands. From interviews that were conducted in Denpasar (capital of Bali) and in Karangasem (rural area in the north) it became clear that particularly older and rural women still are convinced that in principle it is fair that women do not inherit because

[49] Interview on 22 October 2012 with the 49-year-old male Head of the Legal Office of Bali Province in Denpasar.

[50] Windia, 2010, p. 136.

[51] NGO representatives on 24 October 2012. A 39-year-old divorcee explained that she had only dared asking for a divorce from her abusive husband – who is a rich medical specialist – because she was convinced that she would get half of the marital community. She went to the District Court in Denpasar, but did not get her share. Although she found a job, her income is so low that she cannot afford a lawyer to appeal. Her ex-husband got custody over two of their three children; she got custody over the youngest child. She now rents one room where she lives with her child because she cannot afford better housing. Interview on 28 October 2012.

[52] Interview on 22 October 2012 with 49 year-old male Head of the Legal Office of Bali Province in Denpasar.

they do not bear important responsibilities,[53] while many younger, urban, and educated people, think that Adat law needs to be changed.[54]

Especially in Karangasem, where women rise at 4 a.m. to go to the market, work on the land, perform their daily rituals of praying and offering before they start on their household or other chores, it seems surprising that women's responsibilities go largely unnoticed. Also the enormous work women do in preparation of village or family ceremonies – which take place on a regular basis – is largely underestimated and not valued as much as the part that men play in religious rituals. Furthermore, there is a persistent myth that a married woman no longer performs duties in her own family, while in fact, many women take up (religious) responsibilities in the family of their husband and continue their obligations in the family of their blood relatives.[55]

Women are hugely under-represented in decision-making organs. Although there are no formal barriers, women are not represented in local decision-making organs, and none of the village-heads is female.[56] This means that the direct influence of women on creating or changing Adat law is very limited.

4.3. HINDU WOMEN'S LAND RIGHTS; NEW DEVELOPMENTS

The last few decades, Balinese society has been changing on account of several influences, among which democracy, tourism, modern media, and active campaigns by NGOs.[57] Girls and women participate in education, also at university level. Because of the use of birth control, many families, especially in urban areas, are small which increases the chance that there will be no son.[58] While older people, especially women in rural areas, may not be aware of the legal

---

53 Interview with 53-year-old business woman on 10 October 2012 in Denpasar. Interviews with 51-year-old female academic, 55-year-old market woman, and 75-year-old widow on 27 October 2012 in Karangasem.

54 In Denpasar: interview on 2 October 2012 with 57-year-old male professor of Adat law, on 10 October 2012 with 53-year-old business woman, on 11 October 2012 with 56-year-old widow. In Karangasem on 27 October 2012 with 21-year-old female law student, on 28 October 2012: with 39-year-old female pharmacist's assistant, 56-year-old male CEO of a bank, 39-year-old female general practitioner, 17-year-old male pupil.

55 This was observed by the author, but also emphasized by a 53-year-old business woman who felt that if this would be acknowledged, the status of daughters would become better.

56 NGO representatives on 24 October 2012. A 32-year-old male teacher explained that many men feel that female representation is not necessary since the women's fathers and husbands will take women's needs and wishes into account when decisions are made. Interview in Denpasar, 12 October 2012.

57 NGO representatives on 24 October 2012.

58 The birth control programme has been very successful in Bali among the Hindu population. Interview general practitioner, 27 October 2012.

rules and consequences of the Adat law on property, marriage, and inheritance,[59] many educated people – men and women alike – particularly in urban areas are aware that women are discriminated against and many struggle with the fact that girls and women are in an inferior position as regards property rights. Many parents of daughters want to make arrangements for them, but it is not always easy or feasible to give daughters a part of the estate during their lifetime.[60] Couples who worry about what will happen to the wife should she become a widow, may put property acquired during marriage in the wife's name only.[61] Women who receive money from their parents secure property that they put in their own name.[62]

From the interviews that were conducted the picture emerges of a community in which many members are worried about the future of their daughters, wives, and sisters. Different individual solutions are sought, but people seem to be very hesitant to make a concerted effort to influence the existing Adat law for fear of undermining Hindu identity. Women are torn between their personal needs and worries and loyalty to their family, community, and culture.

Under pressure from (women's) NGOs and academics specialized in Adat law,[63] the highest authority for Balinese Adat law, the *Pasamuhan Agung* (General Assembly) of the *Majelis Utama Desa Pakraman Bali* (Supreme Assembly of the Village Council) has adopted a Decree to change the position of women in marital and inheritance law.[64] As has already been mentioned above, the Decree stipulates that women who are in a *biasa* (normal) marriage, are entitled to half of the marriage community, also after divorce. Furthermore, the Decree reiterates the already existing custom that if there are no sons in a family, it is possible that a daughter marries *nyentana/nyeburin*, which means that the woman takes

59 From interviews on 27 and 28 October 2012 in Karangasem, it became clear that older women/widows were not aware of the content or consequences of Adat law; they completely relied on their husbands and sons.

60 Interviews 55-year-old male expert in agrarian law on 5 October 2012, 53-year-old business woman on 10 October 2012, 56-year-old female lecturer in Adat law, 54-year-old female lecturer polytechnic on 23 October 2012, 51-year-old female lecturer in law on 27 October 2012, 21-year-old female law student on 27 October 2012, 39-year-old female pharmacist's assistant on 28 October 2012, 49-year-old female kitchen help on 28 October 2012, 56-year-old male CEO of a bank on 28 October 2012, 39-year-old female general practitioner on 28 October 2012, 17-year-old male pupil on 28 October 2012, 30-year-old female civil servant on 1 November 2012.

61 Interviews with 54-year-old female lecturer polytechnic on 23 October 2012, 49-year-old female kitchen help on 28 October 2012, 56-year-old male CEO of a bank on 28 October 2012.

62 Interviews with 53-year-old business woman on 10 October 2012, 51-year-old female lecturer in law on 27 October 2012, 52-year-old housewife on 27 October 2012.

63 Interview with Wayan Windia, professor of Adat law on 2 October 2012, who was present at the meeting of the General Assembly and who wrote an advice for the MUDP Bali.

64 Decree No 01/Kep/Psm-3/MDP Bali/X/2010, Majelis Utama Desa Pakraman Bali, Denpasar, 15 October 2010.

the status of patrilineal kinship, while her husband becomes part of her family and severs his ties with his blood relatives, which also includes that he no longer has the traditional responsibilities towards his own family. This construction secures that the property will remain in the bride's nuclear family and will not be passed on to her father's nephew(s) when he dies. However, when the prospective bridegroom is an only child, his family will be very reluctant to let him enter into a *nyentana/nyeburin* marriage. That is why a third form of marriage has been devised, the *pada gelahang*. This form of marriage was also sanctioned by the *Pasamuhan Agung* in the Decree, and it entails that both marriage partners get a double status and have rights and obligations in respect of both families.

As regards inheritance law, the Decree stipulates that both sons and daughters are entitled to the marital community of their parents, i.e. only the property that has been accrued by both parents during their marriage. One-third of this property will be deducted and put under the control – not ownership – of the son who will take over the family responsibilities from the parents. The rest of the community will be divided in the following way: each son will get a portion or half of the estate, while each daughter will get half of the estate received by her brother(s).[65] Obviously, this is not in conformity with the principle of equality and it only concerns a small part of the property, excluding the father's family land, but it is an important step forward that daughters for the first time are entitled to part of the estate of their parents according to Adat law.

4.4. REMEDIES

If there is a dispute over land, it is easy and cheap to go through the extensive Adat settlement system. In first instance, a person can approach the *banjar* (neighbourhood), where a case is heard by a group of elders. If the *banjar* cannot offer a solution, the case will be heard by the *Desa Pakraman* (village council). The next step is the *Majelis Desa Pakraman (MDP)* (Assembly of Village Councils), followed by the *Majelis Utama Desa Pakraman (MUDP)* (Supreme Assembly of the Village Councils) of Bali Province. If parties still have not reached a settlement, they can bring their case before the relevant District Court (State Judicial Board).[66] The organs of the settlement system will only apply Adat law so in many cases it is quite predictable that the settlement will not be in a woman's

65 Decree No 01, Chapter III, I (4 and 5), p. 43.

66 I Wayan Koti Cantika, 'Tata Cara Penerapan Pamidanda' (Application Procedures of Punishment), in: I Ketut Sudantra, and A.A. Gede Oka Parwata (eds.), *Wicara Lan Pamidanda* (Conflict and Sanction in Bali's Adat Law), Udayana University Press, Denpasar 2010, p. 101 and I Gusti Agung Putu Yadnya, 'Penyelesaian Perkara Adat; Beberapa Pokok Pikiran (The Settlement of Adat Cases: Some Key Thoughts), in: I Ketut Sudantra and A.A. Gede Oka Parwata (eds.), *Wicara Lan Pamidanda*, Udayana University Press, Denpasar 2010, p. 151.

favour.[67] It is possible to skip the Adat system and go directly to the District Court. However, this is frowned upon because disputes should be settled in harmony, on the basis of kinship and togetherness, and in addition a procedure before the District Court costs money.[68] Moreover, the District Court may decide to apply Adat law because when the claimant is a Balinese Hindu, a representative of the *Majelis Desa Pakraman* will be invited to be present as an expert witness and adviser.[69] While in theory it would be possible to appeal to a General Court, next to the General High Court and in last instance, the Supreme Court, in practice this is a lengthy and very costly procedure that only the affluent can afford. If women lose their case in the District Court, generally they will lack the financial means to take their case any further.[70]

5. UGANDA – INTERNATIONAL AND NATIONAL LEGAL FRAMEWORK

5.1. INTRODUCTION

The question of land rights in Uganda is historically complex and politically sensitive. Land has always had an important role in Ugandan societies: not merely as a source of livelihood, but also from a spiritual and political point of view.[71]

Uganda's land tenure system as we know it today is highly influenced by its colonial legacy. In its quest to gain control of Uganda's productive resources the British Administration implemented a preference-based system, striking deals with local leaders to expand their political base of support.[72] Whilst the British Administration largely upheld the existing societal structures, it also invented new 'traditional' institutions[73] and implemented novel administrative layers

67 The level of education of Desa Adat community leaders may be very low and in many cases they do not understand that their local laws (*awig-awig*) are no longer in conformity with provincial Adat law. Interview on 24 October 2012 with NGO representatives.

68 I Gusti Agung, 2010, pp. 151–152.

69 I Gusti Agung, 2010, p. 156.

70 NGO representatives on 24 October 2012, who claimed that judges sometimes refuse to accept changes in Adat law and instead apply traditional rules.

71 Associates For Development, 'Issues paper for the National Land Policy, Ministry of Water, Lands and Environment, Land tenure reform project' 2004, http://mokoro.co.uk/wp-content/uploads/issues_paper_NationalLandPolicy.pdf, accessed 4 February 2016, p. 4.

72 C. Foley, 'A guide to property law in Uganda' 2007 *United Nations Human Settlements Programme*, http://mirror.unhabitat.org/pmss/listItemDetails.aspx?publicationID=2444, accessed 4 February 2016, p. 7.

73 The British wanted to maintain the facade of respecting traditional institutions, for instance by retaining the authority of the chiefs ('rwodi'), while at the same time making them tools in their own hands. Chiefs that were sympathetic to or useful the British were appointed. These appointed chiefs could be hereditary clan heads, but they could also just be local policemen or interpreters of some British officials or clerks: R. Mukherjee, *Uganda: An historical accident? Class, Nation, State formation*, Africa World Press, Trenton 1985, pp. 144 & 147–148.

alongside existing ones.[74] Three new forms of land tenure were developed by the British Administration besides the system of customary tenure, namely the systems of freehold,[75] mailo[76] and leasehold.[77]

Uganda gained independence from Great Britain on 9 October 1962. During the first decade after independence – under the rule of Milton Obote – the land tenure system was largely left untouched.[78] Under the rule of Idi Amin (1971–1973) rigorous land reforms took place, aimed at giving the Government of Uganda greater control over the use and management of land.[79] However, these reforms were reversed with the adoption of the new Constitution in 1995 and the Land Act in 1998.[80]

This section will first briefly go into the international legal rules that are applicable to Uganda and subsequently it will examine the national legal framework.

5.2. INTERNATIONAL LEGAL FRAMEWORK

Uganda became a party to the Women's Convention in 1985, to the ICESCR in 1987, and to the ICCPR and its Optional Protocol (regarding the individual complaints procedure) in 1995.

At the regional level, Uganda became a party to the African Charter on Human and Peoples' Rights (Banjul Charter) in 1986, to its Protocol on the Establishment of an African Court on Human and Peoples' Rights in 2001, and to the Protocol on the Rights of Women in Africa (Maputo Protocol) in 2010. Uganda is also a signatory to the African Union Solemn Declaration on Gender Equality in Africa.

Some of the most relevant provisions of the international legal instruments were already discussed in Section 2 of this paper. Regarding the binding regional legal instruments, the African Charter on Human and Peoples' Rights contains

---

74 E.g. the establishment of Local Councils & Local Council Courts: Girling, 1960, p. 195.

75 Full ownership rights, see Section 3(2) 1998 Land Act of Uganda for a full definition.

76 A quasi-freehold system, which can be found in the Central Region and parts of central Western Uganda; A. Bomuhangi, C. Doss and R. Meizen-Dick, 'Who Owns the Land?, Perspectives from Rural Ugandans and Implications for Land Acquisitions', 2011 *International Food Policy Research Centre*, www.ifpri.org/publication/who-owns-land, accessed 4 February 2016, p. 6. See also Section 3(4) of the 1998 Land Act of Uganda for a definition.

77 A form of tenure under which one person grants or is deemed to have granted another person exclusive possession of land usually but not necessarily for a period defined, directly or indirectly, by reference to a specific date of commencement and a specific date of ending. See for a full definition Section 3(5) 1998 Land Act.

78 Associates For Development, 2004, p. 6. Although a legal instrument was adopted that slightly strengthened the position of those holding land under the system of customary tenure, namely the Public Lands Act of 1969: Foley, 2007, p. 8.

79 The Idi Amin Government passed the land reform decree 1975, which *inter alia* declared all land in Uganda to be publicly owned and centrally vested with the Ugandan Land Commission.

80 Foley, 2007, p. 10.

relevant provisions concerning the equal enjoyment of the rights of the Charter,[81] equality and equal protection before the law,[82] the right to participate in government,[83] and the right to property.[84]

The Maputo Protocol contains provisions for the promotion and protection of the rights of women in a number of areas, including the right to property. The Protocol goes further than the Women's Convention in scope of protected rights and deals with rights already covered in the Women's Convention with more specificity.[85] It explicitly addresses different categories of women like married women or divorced women, widows, women in economic activities and the informal sector, and elderly women.[86]

Since no relevant reservations have been made to the international or regional conventions,[87] the provisions on non-discrimination and equality fully apply in respect of the obligations of the State and all its organs. However, since Uganda has a dualist legal system, international law needs to be incorporated into national law, before any rights ensuing from it become justiciable at the national level.

5.3. NATIONAL LEGAL FRAMEWORK

The formal legal framework on land tenure in Uganda is made up of the 1995 Constitution and the 1998 Land Act.

5.3.1. The Constitution

The Ugandan Constitution is the supreme law of the State. It has binding force on all authorities and persons throughout Uganda. If any other law or any custom is inconsistent with any of the provisions of the Constitution, the Constitution shall prevail and that other law or custom shall be void to the extent of the inconsistency.[88]

---

81 Article 2.

82 Article 3. Article 18 on the rights of the family contains a paragraph specifically on the rights of women and children: '3. *the state shall ensure the elimination of every discrimination against women and also ensure the protection of the rights of women and the child as stipulated in international declarations and conventions.*'

83 Article 13.

84 Article 14.

85 F. Viljoen, 'An introduction to the Protocol to the African Charter on Human and Peoples' Rights on the Rights of Women in Africa' in *Wash. & Lee J.C.R. & Soc. Just (Washington and Lee Journal of Civil Rights and Social Justice)*, Vol. 16, Issue 1, 2009, p. 21.

86 See Articles 6, 7, 13(e) and (f), 20–22.

87 Reservations were made with regard to clauses 14 and 21 of the Maputo Protocol on abortion.

88 Article 2, 1995 Constitution of Uganda.

Relevant to the land rights of women is that the Constitution contains provisions on the equal rights of women.[89] It also contains provisions on affirmative action in favour of marginalised groups.[90] Regarding land rights, the Ugandan Constitution specifically provides for 'protection from deprivation of property.'[91] In a separate chapter on '*Land and Environment*' it sets out fairly detailed provisions in relation to land rights.[92] Under the Constitution customary tenure is recognized as one of four tenure systems under which a person can have property rights over land.[93]

5.3.2. The 1998 Land Act

The 1998 Land Act builds upon and further elaborates the provisions of the Constitution,[94] whereby the two main issues are ownership and tenure rights and land administration.[95] While customary tenure was already explicitly recognized as a form of property rights over land under the Constitution, the Land Act recognizes customary law as the regulatory framework for this tenure system.[96] It also includes sections that increase protection of the rights of women to own, use and inherit land. However, at the same time not all legal hurdles for the attainment of *de facto* equality on land rights have been taken. For instance, Article 22 of the Land Act reads: '*(...) For the purpose of holding land under customary tenure, a family shall be deemed to be a legal person represented by the head of the family.*'[97] Since traditionally men are seen as heads of family rather than women, this causes substantive inequality.[98] The Committee on the Elimination of Discrimination Against Women (CEDAW) in its Concluding Observations of October 2010 (with respect to Article 14 on rural women) urged Uganda '*to eliminate all forms of discrimination with respect to the ownership, co-sharing and inheritance of land.*' It further urged '*the introduction of measures to address negative customs and traditional practices, especially in rural areas, which affect full enjoyment of the right to property by women.*' The African Commission on Human and Peoples' Rights was also critical with regard to the provisions on land rights. In its Concluding Observations of November 2011 it expressed its concern that the

---

89 Article 33.
90 Article 32.
91 Article 26.
92 Chapter 15.
93 Article 237(3): 'The land tenure systems under which land can be owned according to this provision are: (a) customary; (b) freehold; (c) mailo; and(d) leasehold'.
94 As amended by Land Amendment Acts 2001, 2004, and 2010.
95 Foley, 2007, p. 12.
96 Section 3(1) 1998 Land Act.
97 An earlier draft of the Land Act contained a clause that would allow spouses to co-own property went 'missing' in the final draft of the act: Asiimwe, p. 2, 3, and 8.
98 Also, activists have campaigned for reforms to Uganda's property laws to provide for spouses to be deemed co-owners of 'family land', *i.e.* land on which the married couple lives and on which they depend: F. Benedetti and Helen Kijo-Bisimba, 'Women's rights in Uganda: gaps between policy and practice' 2012 International Federation for Human Rights (FIDH) https://www.fidh.org/IMG/pdf/uganda582afinal.pdf, accessed 4 February 2016, p. 22.

earlier recommendation to adopt measures to ensure the effective protection of the rights of indigenous populations by establishing laws that protect land rights and natural resources of indigenous populations had not been complied with.[99]

5.3.2. *National Land Policy*

After an inclusive and consultative process that stretched over more than a decade,[100] a new Ugandan National Land Policy was gazetted in August 2013. The goal of this policy is '*to ensure an efficient, equitable and optimal utilization and management of Uganda's land resources for poverty reduction, wealth creation and overall socio-economic development*'.[101] The policy addresses the vast majority of outstanding issues regarding Uganda's land legislation.[102] It recognizes that perhaps the most critical and challenging element of Uganda's land question has to do with disentangling the multiple and conflicting tenure rights and interests often overlapping in respect of the same plot of land.[103]

5.3.4. *Other relevant legal instruments and organs*

Concerning women's rights, major pieces of legislation have come into force in Uganda in recent years, namely the Domestic Violence Act and the Prohibition of Female Genital Mutilation Act. Uganda has a National Gender Policy and gender issues have been mainstreamed into other government policies,[104] such as the National Development Plan.[105] Uganda has a Human Rights Commission since 1995 and in July 2010 the Government officially launched the 'Equal Opportunities Commission'.[106] Overall, Uganda has been hailed for its progressive legislation

---

99 Concluding Observations of the African Commission on Human and Peoples' Rights on the 4th periodic report of the Republic of Uganda (presented at the 49th ordinary session of the African Commission on Human and Peoples' Rights held in Banjul, The Gambia from 28 April to 12 May 2011), Part IV.

100 M. Rugadya, 'Developing a National Land Policy in Uganda: A Learning Process' *Rural Development Institute* 2015, www.landesa.org/wp-content/uploads/National-Land-Policy-in-Uganda_A-Learning-Process_-FINAL.pdf, accessed 4 February 2016, p. 2.

101 Uganda National Land Policy, Chapter 2.3.

102 C. Burke and D.N. Kobusingiye, 'Women's Land Rights in Northern Uganda – Securing Women's Land Rights in Northern Uganda Report' *commissioned by Oxfam* 2014, www.landcoalition.org/sites/default/files/documents/resources/Securing%20Women%20Land%20Rights%20Report_with%20covers%20_0.pdf, accessed 4 February 2016, p. 15.

103 National land policy, p 1.

104 The National Gender policy 2007 of the Republic of Uganda. The policy is meant to serve as a '*guide to all stakeholders in planning, resource allocation, implementation and monitoring and evaluation of programmes with a gender perspective*'.

105 Uganda National Development plan, 2010/2011–2014/2015.

106 The Human Rights Commission was established under Article 51 of the 1995 Constitution of Uganda. The Equal Opportunities Commission is a statutory body established by an Act of Parliament to effectuate Article 32(3) and Article 32(4) of the Constitution. The functions of the Commission according to Article 14 of the 2007 Equal opportunities Commission Act are to monitor evaluate compliance by various actors (State as well as non-State actors) '*with*

and institutions in the field of gender equality.[107] However, discriminatory laws are still in place, hampering the materialisation of the right to equality for women in Uganda. For example, women do not have equal rights under the 1904 Marriage Act nor under the 1906 Succession Act. Under the Succession Act for instance, women cannot inherit their father's property. In 2006 a couple of women's rights organizations successfully petitioned the Constitutional Court to declare this provision unconstitutional.[108] Nonetheless, the Succession Act has not been reformed until now and several provisions that contravene women's rights in the Marriage Act and in the Succession Act remain effective.[109]

The African Commission on Human and Peoples' Rights in its Concluding Observations of November 2011 recommended that Uganda: '*takes measures to pass a specific law domesticating the Maputo Protocol*'.[110] In its Fifth Periodic Report of 25 September 2013, regarding the period 2010–2012, the Government of Uganda submitted that steps were already being undertaken to domesticate many of the Maputo Protocol's provisions. It remains to be seen if and when the recommendations of the ACHPR are going to be fully complied with.

In spite of the abovementioned legislative hurdles, the obstacles to the improvement of women's rights in Uganda do not lie mainly in the legal

equal opportunities and affirmative action in favour of groups marginalized on the basis of sex, race, colour, ethnic origin, tribe, creed, religion, social or economic standing, political opinion, disability, gender, age or any other reason created by history, tradition or custom'.

107 See e.g. Rachel Spighiger, Rikke Brandt Broegaard, Rasmus Hundsbæk Pedersen and Helle Munk Ravnborg, 'Land administration, gender equality and development cooperation Lessons learned and challenges ahead' *Danish Institute for International Studies* 2013 www.diis.dk/en/research/land-rights-gender-equality-and-donor-cooperation accessed 04-02-2016, p. 45.

108 Law Advocacy for Women in Uganda v Attorney General – Constitutional Petitions Nos. 13 /05 /& 05 /06 [2007] UGCC 1 (5 April 2007); See also F. Benedetti and Helen Kijo-Bisimba, 2012, p. 22.

109 A marriage and divorce bill, meant to replace the Marriage Act and the Succession Act, was carried forward to Parliament in 2009. One of the key elements addressed by this bill is the issue of women's rights during marriage and particularly the right to own property both within and after a marriage has been dissolved. According to the Government of Uganda, this bill was further subjected to countrywide consultation and reports are yet to be submitted back to Parliament. Nevertheless, the bill is still on the order paper of Parliament, Fifth periodic report presented to the African Commission on Human and Peoples' Rights at the 54rd ordinary session held in Banjul, the Gambia 22 October–5 November 2013 by the Government of Uganda, www.achpr.org/files/sessions/54th/state-reports/5-2010-2012/periodic_report_2010_2012_eng.pdf, accessed 4 February 2016, p. 13. In some areas legislation relevant to the rights of women even seems to be having an adverse effect. In February 2014 the anti-pornography act was adopted. It makes 'the act of pornography' an offence. The rationale behind it is that 'pornography' leads to sexual crimes against women and children including rape, child molestation and incest. However, in practice the act has led to the harassment and mistreatment of women in public, due to the vague and broad definition of pornography, which includes 'indecent show (...) for primarily sexual excitement'.

110 On the Rights of Women in Africa; Concluding Observations on the 4th periodic report of the Republic of Uganda, regarding the period 2008–2010, presented at the 49th Ordinary Session of the ACHPR held in Banjul, the Gambia from 28 April to 12 May 2011, p. 6.

framework, but more in a lack of implementation of the existing laws, which remains limited. Hindrances to the achievement of *de facto* improvement include an inadequate budget and a lack of awareness and skills among Government officials and the judiciary.[111] Other obstacles concern access to justice, an issue that will be discussed in the next section.

6. SITUATION IN ACHOLI

6.1. BACKGROUND

Acholi, also referred to as 'Acholiland', is a Subregion of the Northern region of Uganda. Its inhabitants are mainly from the Acholi people.[112] Acholi society is generally a rural patriarchal society. Most families depend on land for their livelihoods. It is estimated that at least 90% of the land in Acholi is possessed under a system of customary tenure,[113] which means that the landholders do not have a formal title to the land that they use.

Acholi society is divided into small polities or chiefdoms each of which consists of a number of villages[114] that are made up of different patrilineal clans.[115] Within the chiefdom there is (at least) one royal aristocratic clan headed by the clan chief (rwot moo). The other clans within the chiefdom are referred to as commoner clans. These are headed by clan heads, sitting together as council of elders.

[111] In its Country Report of 6 December 2012 to the ICESCR the Government of Uganda describes the main challenges in the overall promotion of gender equality, namely '(a)technical constraints in the form of inadeaquate skills / capacity in all sectors (...); (b)Financial constraints resulting from the fact that gender equality budget allocations have been very low at all levels; (c) Socio-cultural constraints demonstrated by resistance towards gender equality among decision makers, planners and implementers at all levels; and (d) Institutional constraints evidenced lack of an incentive system / boundary system (...)', Country report, para. 34.

[112] The development of a single society with a collective and ethnic identity, to be labelled as 'Acholi', was a process that took around 100–125 years beginning in the late seventeenth century. Before that time Acholiland 'was a multicultural frontier region where Central Sudanic, Eastern Nilotic, and, though to a lesser degree, Luo languages and worlds met.': R.R. Atkinson, *The Roots of Ethnicity – The Origins of the Acholi of Uganda Before 1800*, University of Pennsylvania Press, Philadelphia, 1994, p. 75.

[113] J. Hopwood and R.R. Atkinson, *Land conflict monitoring and mapping tool for the Acholi Sub-region, Final Report*, Research conducted under the United Nations Peacebuilding Programme in Uganda by Human Rights Focus, March 2013, p. 55.

[114] R.R. Atkinson, 1994, p. 75.

[115] I. Anying, *Re-envisioning Gender Justice in Access and use of land through traditional institutions – a case for customary tenure of land ownership in Acholi sub-region, Northern Uganda*, Research partnership programme, Danish Institute for Human Rights (DIHR), 2012, p 25.

Further down the line of hierarchy the clans are subdivided into hamlets and households.[116]

6.2. ACHOLI CUSTOMARY LAW

As mentioned in Section 5.3.1, the Ugandan Constitution explicitly recognizes customary tenure as a system under which a person can have property rights over land.[117] Although there is no uniform version of Acholi customary law[118] some basic rules can be distinguished.[119]

Under Acholi customary law, land is the property of past, current and future generations.[120] It is in other words a 'transgenerational asset'. Traditionally no-one *owns* the land for him- or herself as in the freehold tenure system. Therefore, one usually speaks of access to land rights, rather than ownership rights. Typically plots should be set aside for communal usage, for instance as grazing land; hunting grounds; ceremonial land, etc.[121] Land disputes are dealt with through a process of mediation, whereby the aim is to restore social harmony rather than to provide justice.[122]

Under Acholi customary law the clan elders representing the clan have the responsibility of overseeing administration of all land belonging to the clan. This responsibility includes ensuring the proper use of the land; making certain that heirs are appointed at household level to manage the land; and overseeing and

---

116 F.K. Girling, *The Acholi of Uganda*, Her Majesty's Stationary Office, London, 1960, pp. 7–8; I. Anying, 2012, p 26: '*A hamlet generally consists of a number of households, while a household is regarded as the smallest social unit, typically a husband, wife (or wives), and children.*'

117 Article 237, para. 3: The 1998 Land Act defines customary tenure as follows: '*(...) a form of tenure applicable to a specific area of land and a specific description or class of persons, governed by rules generally accepted as binding and authoritative by a class of persons to which it applies, characterized by local customary regulations and management to individual and household ownership and at the same time providing for communal ownership and use of land*'.

118 Hopwood and Atkinson identified a large variety of significant land practices within Acholi: J. Hopwood and R.R. Atkinson, 2013, p.5.

119 For the purpose of this paper, the 'basic rules' have partly been distilled from the '*Principles and Practices of Customary Tenure in Acholiland*' of June 2008. Although there has been some controversy relating to the participation in the development of this text and the preparation of an alternative version is underway (see C. Burke and D.N. Kobusingiye, 2014, p. 24), it is thought by the authors that the document can nonetheless serve as guidance in identifying some of the core aspects of Acholi customary law.

120 J. Adoko, J. Akin and R. Knight, *Understanding and Strengthening Women's Land Rights Under Customary Tenure in Uganda*, Land and Equity Movement in Uganda (LEMU), April 2011, p. 1.

121 Principles and Practices of Customary Tenure in Acholiland, Part 1, (d); see also F.K. Girling, 1960, pp. 231–232 (Appendix D by R.M. Bere).

122 J. Hopwood, 'Women's Land Claims in the Acholi Region of Northern Uganda: What Can Be Learned from What Is Contested' (2015) *IJMGR (International Journal on Minority and Group Rights)* 22, p. 408.

authorisation any land sales. Heads of the household manage the land on behalf of the family and allocate land for use by the other members of the household. They have the right to use and allocate land, but also the responsibility – as stewards of the land – to ensure the interests of the family. The position of head of household is traditionally held by a man, but can also be held by a woman.[123] Generally, what characterises the Acholi customary tenure system is the fact that those clan members holding management rights with regard to the land, also have corresponding responsibilities, namely to make certain that the land is being used properly and that all clan members are given land rights.[124]

Women always have the right to access land, as illustrated in the table below. Where this land can be accessed depends on their marital status. Prior to marriage, a woman is entitled to access and use land that is her blood relatives' property. After marriage, she is entitled to access and use her husband's family land. If her husband dies, she takes her deceased husband's place as head of the household (and a protector will be appointed whom she may accept or reject). She may also return to her blood relatives' land and she will have the right to access that land. The same situation regarding the return to the homestead applies to a divorced woman.[125]

Category of person	Access to their blood relatives' land	Access to their husband's family's land
Unmarried woman	◆	
Married woman		◆
Widow	◆	◆
Divorced woman	◆	

Although the system of customary tenure is recognized under the Ugandan Constitution, the relationship between the two regulatory systems, namely: the system of statutory law and that of 'customary law' is unclear. There is no question about the Constitution being the primary source of law and the fact that all other laws and regulations need to be in conformity with the Constitution. However, apart from this, the question of how the various provisions relate to each other

123 J. Hopwood and R.R. Atkinson, 2013, p. 51. Female heads of households are for instance widowed women or women who have children without getting married.

124 Principles and Practices of Customary Tenure in Acholiland, Part 2, Section 7. In fact all clan members have responsibilities with regard to the land: See Part 2, Section 4.

125 This description is based on the Principles and Practices of Customary Tenure in Acholiland, Part 2, Sections 2, 6, and 8. It is thought to represent the land rights situation in most, but not necessarily all Acholi communities, since there may great variations in customary tenure systems across the Acholi Sub-region. Research on the topic has so far been too limited to draw any blanket conclusions. See. J. Hopwood and R.R. Atkinson, 2013, p. 7. See also fn. 119. Regarding the acceptance of a divorced woman back into the home of her blood relatives see also J. Hopwood, 2015, p. 403 and F.K. Girling, 1960, pp. 39–40.

with a view to hierarchy is ambiguous. This constitutes a serious problem with regard to women's land rights because uncertainty about the applicable rules plays into the hands of the more powerful.[126]

6.3. ACHOLI WOMEN'S LAND RIGHTS IN PRACTICE

6.3.1. *The current situation*

Since Acholi society is patriarchal in nature, the Acholi customary law inherently favours men with regard to land rights. The system does not prevent women from accessing land. Generally, it also does not prevent women from holding senior positions within the clan.[127] However, the system's main building blocks are family units within which the male members of family are heads of household. As heads of household men are by default the ones who manage the land and thus the ones who have stronger land rights.

This fact is of major importance with regard to the alienation or sale of land. If a man wants to bequeath or sell land to someone outside the clan, he needs permission from the extended family and the clan. However, if a woman wishes to do so, she not only needs permission from the extended family and clan, but also from her husband or father.[128]

Other difficulties that seem to be common are to do with the effectuation of the land rights of widows. A widow has a strong position under Acholi customary law. She 'inherits' the position of head of household, which means she is entitled to manage the land of the household. However, in practice this theoretically strong position may actually cause her to become the target of abuse by the male relatives of the deceased husband.[129] If she and the children are not physically present on the husband's family's land, they put their inheritance rights at risk since they may lose their land claims to land grabbing relatives. For some men, *e.g.* brothers of the deceased husband, this forms an incentive to abuse the widow in order to make her leave. At the same time a widow is prone to stay on the

---

126 Attaining clarity with regard to the law is now one of the spearheads of the new National Land Policy, see The Uganda National Land Policy, 02–2013, Chapter 2.4.

127 C. Burke and E. Egaru, *Identification of Good Practice in Land Conflict Resolution in Acholi*, United Nations Resident Coordinator's Office (UNRCO), November 2011, p. 120.

128 C. Burke and D.N. Kobusingiye, 2014, p. 27 (the report describes the land rights situation of women under customary law across Northern Uganda, including Acholi).

129 Regarging attempts by in-laws to evict widows as a common phenomenon see J. Hopwood, 2015, p. 403.

husband's family's land, even when she is subjected to severe mental or physical abuse in order to safeguard the rights of her children.[130]

Also, as it is presumed that a girl will eventually get married, the allocation of land to unmarried women is usually temporal. A woman who returns after her marriage breaks down or after she becomes widowed, may have rights to land at her blood relatives' property, but in some cases family members are reluctant to return the right to access to land to these women.[131]

In spite of the challenges mentioned above as regards Acholi women's land rights and perhaps contrary to expectations, one can say that in general women have quite a strong land rights position. According to a recent study by Burke and Kobusingye on the land rights of women in Northern Uganda (including Acholi), the great majority of women in Acholi do in fact have access to land.[132]

Generally, where clan structures are solid, women's land rights are protected.[133] For instance, a strong clan will not easily permit the titling of land in the name of male heads of family since land is supposed to stay within the clan. It is of course essential for the effectuation of land rights that clan elders have sufficient knowledge with regard to the applicable customary rules. As noted in the introduction to this paper, Acholi society has been subjected to a devastating armed conflict in recent years. Not only did this cause damage to clan structures and lead to demoralisation of the society, it also caused a breakdown of the knowledge base within the clans. Problems regarding the effectuation of women's

---

130 J. Adoko, J. Akin and R. Knight, 'Understanding and Strengthening Women's Land Rights Under Customary Tenure in Uganda', Land and Equity Movement in Uganda (LEMU), 2011, p. 3.

131 C. Burke and D.N. Kobusingiye, 2014, p. 21: Usually, in case of divorce the woman returns to the brother whose wedding was paid with the dowry of the woman's wedding.

132 C. Burke and D.N. Kobusingiye, 2014, p. 28: Regarding Northern Uganda as a whole 63% of the women surveyed reported to have property rights over land and 86% of women held that they have access under customary tenure. (p. 53) The findings were based on interviews with approximately 1200 respondents; 21 focused group discussions and interviews with over 60 key respondents across northern Uganda in the districts of Koboko, Moyo, Kitgum, Lira, Soroti and Kaabong. (p. 2) Regarding the district that lies in Acholi: 'Kitgum', the findings were that 83 percent of the respondents alleged they 'owned' land (p. 28), which could probably best be understood as the *'act, state or right of posession'* rather than the right to alienate (sell, mortgage or transfer) land. (pp. 27–28); The conclusions from the study by Burke and Kobusingiye are supported by the findings of J. Hopwood and R.R. Atkinson in their research: *Land conflict monitoring and mapping tool for the Acholi Sub-region, Final Report*, Research conducted under the United Nations Peacebuilding Programme in Uganda by Human Rights Focus, 03.2013, p. iv.

133 Telephonic interview with Julian Hopwood, Gulu (Uganda) based researcher & currently PhD candidate at Ghent University, on 24 January 2014.

land rights seem to arise mainly where clan structures are weakened and where power is not in balance.[134]

6.3.2. *Concerns for the future*

On the basis of its policy of agricultural liberalisation the Government of Uganda has aimed for the transferral of customary property rights to freehold tenure for the past few decades.[135] One of the assumptions that usually underlie agricultural modernisation efforts is that a 'freehold' system (with titles) provides better security to the titleholders and is therefore a vehicle for agricultural growth.[136] Therefore, the transferal of customarily owned land to private 'freehold tenure' has been widely promoted.[137] The 1998 Land Act contains the legal framework to enable such transferral: On the basis of the Land Act it is possible to register customarily owned land by which a certificate of customary ownership (CCO) is obtained.[138] Direct transferral from customarily owned land to privately owned land is also possible on the basis of the Land Act. However, when a CCO has already been issued, conversion of the title of the land in question from the customary to the freehold tenure regime is relatively easy.[139] However, as many stakeholders now contend, the underlying assumption – that a freehold title provides better security- does not hold true in many cases. Most of the land in Uganda held under customary tenure is not held by individuals, but by communities or families. The

---

134 Telephonic interview with Julian Hopwood on 24 January 2014; See also Burke and Kobusingiye, 2014, p. 18: '*When [the respondents of our research] were questioned on what they mean by the "strength" of the family or clan very few people referred to the physical size of the family. The majority of respondents referred to the financial resources at the family's disposal and levels of education while others spoke of "love", "unity" or "cohesion" within the family institution.*'

135 A policy of agricultural liberalisation was initiated by the Government of Uganda in 1987: N. Bazaara, 'Impact of liberalisation on agriculture and food security in Uganda' Structural Adjustment Participatory Review Initiative Final report, 2001 www.saprin.org/uganda/research/uga_liberalization.pdf accessed 4 February 2016, p. 9. Since the mid-80s the Ugandan Government, under influence from the World Bank, made land tenure reform its priority agenda. After debating the issue for over 10 years a land policy was formed, reflected in the relevant provisions of the 1995 Constitution and the 1998 Land Act. These legal instruments facilitate the transferral of customary land tenure ship to freehold tenure, while not providing for the reverse transferral of freehold to customary tenure: J. Mugambwa, 'A comparative analysis of land tenure law reform in Uganda and Papua New Guinea' (2007) *JSPL (Journal of South Pacific Law)* 11(1), pp. 52–53.

136 Land and Equity Movement Uganda (LEMU), 'Linking Land Tenure and Agricultural Modernisation: Making PMA relevant for all', undated, www.land-in-uganda.org/assets/Info.%20Paper%20Land%20Tenure%20and%20Agricultural%20Modernisation.pdf, accessed 4 February 2016, p. 1.

137 J. Hopwood, 2015, p. 388.

138 Section 4 1998 Land Act of Uganda.

139 Section 11 of the Land Act reads: '(...) Any person who holds a certificate of customary ownership shall be exempted in respect of that land from the verification described by section 5'. Section 5 concerns the determination of rights over the land, such as titleholders, boundaries rights of occupation or use.

possibility to transfer customarily owned land to 'freehold tenure' may induce some family heads to treat land as their personal property, hereby denying other family members their rights. Once land is titled in the name of the family head on the basis of the Land Act, this family head – usually a male person – has a far greater power over the land.[140]

Although the 'CCO topic' is high on the agendas of those working in the field of land rights in Northern Uganda,[141] the registration of customary ownership (or subsequent transferral of a CCO to a freehold title) does not yet seem to be a major practice in Acholi at this point in time.[142] This may to a large extent be due to the fact that the bodies for the administration of land rights are barely operational in Acholi.[143] As cited earlier, an estimated 90 percent of the land in Acholi is still held under a system of customary tenure.

6.4. REMEDIES

If an Acholi woman's rights are infringed upon, she may – depending on the level at which the infringement has risen – seek a resolution within her clan; either at household, hamlet, or clan level.[144] She may also try to find remedy at the Acholi Cultural Institution 'Ker Kwaro Acholi' or at the Local Council Court.

---

140 Section 22 of the 1998 Land Act reads: '(...) For the purpose of holding land under customary tenure, a family shall be deemed to be a legal person represented by the head of the family.' Since the head of the family is traditionally expected to be a male person this may disadvantage women in practice.

141 The topic was raised as a major concern by a couple of interviewed NGO-representatives; A concern that was frequently uttered refers to the question of who to include on the CCO. The issue is not only which family members to include, but – since customarily owned land is seen as a transgenerational asset – the question arises of how to register the 'future generations'. Also, more in general, a system of registration of ownership without equal access to education for both sexes and without proper monitoring and registration bodies, will only favour the strong and educated. This will be to the detriment of the rural women.

142 'Only in recent years has the government taken steps to delineate the process for ensuring this right. In 2012, newly established Area Land Committees (ALCs) began accepting applications for Certificates of Customary Ownership (CCOs)': J. Shewan, 'Certificates of Customary Ownership: A Roundtable Discussion on Perceptions, Implications, and Challenges With Stakeholders from Acholi Sub-region' 2012 *Refugee Law Project* http://refugeelawproject.org/files/ACCS_activity_briefs/Certificates_of_Customary_Ownership.pdf, accessed 4 February 2016, p. 1.

143 On the basis of Article 4 of the 1998 Land Act a CCO may be issued by the District Land Board upon submission of the application to the Land Area Committee. The Land Committee plays an important role in the process of registration since it is tasked with determining, verifying and marking the boundaries of all interests in the land which is the subject of the application: Article 5 1998 Land Act.

144 See para 6.1 for a short explanation of the terms household and hamlet.

The Ker Kwaro Acholi[145] is an organization that was set up in 2000 under the terms of Article 246 of the 1995 Constitution of Uganda.[146] In accordance with the Constitution and the 1998 Land Act, this 'institution of traditional or cultural leaders' may determine disputes over customary tenure, or act as mediator between persons who are in dispute over any matters arising out of customary tenure.[147] However, recently the activities of the Ker Kwaro Acholi were put on hold, due to allegations of corruption.[148]

Another institution at the (semi-)informal level that a woman could turn to is that of the Local Council Courts. Local Council Courts have competence to adjudicate certain matters of law, with the exception of most criminal matters. These Local Council Courts actually make up a (quasi) judicial institution that is formally recognized by the Ugandan Constitution as being part of the Judiciary. Local Council Courts were established in 1988 by the Government of Uganda with the aim of replacing the lower level Magistrate courts which had the authority to deal with land rights issues. The LC courts, 'LCCs', were intended to be less formal and to facilitate the improvement of access to justice for all people in Uganda, especially the poor and vulnerable. Local leaders would be enabled to deliver justice to their own communities by drawing both on formal legal principles and customary law.[149] Top-down, they are structured as LCCIII (sub-county level), LCCII (Parish level) and LCCI (village level). The LCCs are monitored by the Chief Magistrates, who can adjudicate over appeals of LCCs' decisions.[150]

Although it may not be usual for a(n) (rural) Acholi woman to step out of the informal structures, she has the possibility to take a case regarding a land dispute to a Magistrates Court as well.[151] The main barriers with regard to the formal

---

145 'authority of Acholi traditional grandfathers /elders': T. Allen, 'Bitter Roots: The Invention of Acholi Traditional Justice' in T. Allen and K. Vlassenroot (eds.), *The Lord's Resistance Army: Myth and Reality*, Zed Books, London 2010, p. 248.

146 Ibid.

147 1995 Constitution of Uganda, Chapter Sixteen; 1998 Land Act of Uganda, Article 88(1).

148 Regarding allegations of corruption: Daily Monitor, 'Acholi king in trouble over Shs230m donor fund', 2 December 2013, www.monitor.co.ug/News/National/Acholi-king-in-trouble-over-Shs230m-donor-fund/-/688334/2095108/-/m7rbt5z/-/index.html, accessed 15 April 2015; Hereafter a new Ker Kwaro Acholi prime minister was appointed: Acholi Times, 'Mr. Okin P.P. appointed new Ker Kwaro Acholi prime minister', 8 September 2014, www.acholitimes.com/index.php/acholi-news/2610-mr-okin-p-p-appointed-new-ker-kwaro-acholi-prime-minister, accessed 15 April 2015.

149 J. Hopwood and R.R. Atkinson, 2013, p. 7; C. Foley, 2007, p. 14; E.R. Mwenda *et al.*: *Uganda – Legal and Judicial Sector Study Report*, The World Bank, July 2009, pp. 44–47.

150 E.R. Mwenda *et al*, 2009, p. 44.

151 A Magistrates' Court is the court at the lowest level of the Ugandan formal legal system. From bottom to top the system is organized as Magistrates' Grade I and II; Chief Magistrates' Court; High Court; Court of Appeal, which also functions as the Constitutional Court; Supreme Court; however, According to the earlier mentioned research by C. Burke and D.N. Kobusingiye (2014) on women's land rights in Northern Uganda Magistrates' Courts

justice system are long travel distances;[152] high litigation costs; long duration of procedures, due to the fact that the system is highly overburdened;[153] and even the fact that court proceedings are conducted in English in urban settings, which can be alienating for those coming from rural areas.[154]

The LCCs potentially have many advantages. The LCC-members are closer to the people they serve and therefore they generally have more knowledge about the situation on the ground. Travel distances are less, costs are lower and procedures are quicker. However, on the basis of a Constitutional Court decision of 2006 the LCIs and LCIIs are unconstitutional until new elections have been held.[155] There is confusion about the value of their decisions at this moment. Other challenges are low literacy levels among the LCIs and LCIIs,[156] exploitation and nepotism.[157] Especially where women are vulnerable, they are prone to exploitation by the LCCs.[158]

The advantages and disadvantages of the traditional mechanisms (within the clan or at the cultural institution) for resolving land rights issues are largely similar to those of the LCCs,[159] although the effectiveness of available mechanism varies greatly from area to area. Every sub-region, county and sub-county has its specific challenges. In areas that have been most affected by the conflict, the level of demoralisation and loss of structures is the highest. Also, the Government of Uganda has introduced many new administrative areas, which has not always corresponded with the available legal structures in place, leading to gaps in leadership.[160]

The laws and policies on land rights are not only ambiguous on content of the law, but also on legal process, specifically with regard to the hierarchy of the

have little to no relevance in this context, solving only one percent of land related disputes in northern Uganda.

152 The Magistrates' Courts for the Acholi Sub-region are all situated in Gulu: C. Burke and D.N. Kobusingiye, 2014, p. 46.

153 J. Hopwood and R.R. Atkinson, 2013, p. 9; G. Mckibben D by R.M. Bere), pp. 231–232 (ap. 231–232 (appendixe in relationships outside the village. tier region where Central Sudanic, E and J. Bean, *Land or Else: Land Based Conflict, Vulnerability, and Disintegration in Northern Uganda*, International Organisation for Migration, United Nations Development Fund and Norwegian Refugee Council, 2010, p. 35.

154 M. Llamazares, 2013, p. 43.

155 C. Burke and E, Egaru, 2011, p. 9.

156 C. Burke, 2011, p. 8.

157 M.A. Rugadya, '*Escalating land conflicts in Uganda, a review of evidence from recent studies and surveys*', Uganda Round Table Foundation, June 2009, p. 22.

158 M.A. Rugadya, 2009, p. 22: 'They need gender sensitization as well as education campaigns on human rights.'

159 Sometimes the local council members are even the same as the principals within the traditional justice system.

160 Telephonic interview with Julian Hopwood, Gulu (Uganda) based researcher & currently PhD candidate at Ghent University, on 24 January 2014.

various legal fora. For instance, there is no consensus on the question of which LCC is the court of first instance in land matters (LCI or LCII). Also, regarding the hierarchical structure of all existing legal tribunals, there is confusion. This situation leads to forum shopping by those who can afford it.[161] The ones who suffer the most under unclear laws are those who are already in a weak position, which are more likely to be women than men.

7. ANALYSIS AND POSSIBLE SOLUTIONS

When the land rights of women in Uganda – specifically in Acholi – and in Indonesia – specifically in Bali – are compared, it becomes clear that irrespective of the difference in culture and the geographical distance between the two countries, there are more similarities than differences to be found. In this section, first the differences will be examined after which the similarities will be scrutinized. Subsequently, possible solutions for improvement will be discussed.

7.1. DIFFERENCES

A few differences may be discerned when the two cases are compared. For instance, Balinese Adat law was largely codified in colonial times while Acholi continues to be organized on a largely communal basis.[162] In Acholi, the principles of customary law on land are therefore essentially negotiable.[163]

If the two communities are compared, it becomes clear that Acholi is largely an agricultural society. Although agriculture is also important in Bali, tourism is the principal source of income. The tourist industry affects the population's land rights in a negative way because it has caused an increase in the price of land and it has made land scarce since it is claimed for hotels, resorts, roads and other facilities. In addition, land is needed for the influx of poor Javanese people especially in the Western part of Bali who wish to settle permanently on the

161 C. Burke and D.N. Kobusingiye, 2014, p.22.

162 F.K. Girling refers to an attempt at the recording of Acholi customary law during the colonial era by the District Commissioner of Acholi, 'Postlethwaite': F.K. Girling, 1960, p. 85; However these texts remained unpublished: J. Hopwood, 2015, p. 394; A recent attempt by the by the officially recognized Acholi cultural institution, 'Ker Kwaro Acholi' (representing the pre-colonial chiefdoms or domains) to codify Acholi customary rules on land in the form of 'Principles, Practices, Rights and Responsibilities', was not broadly accepted. The main criticism concerned: 1) the limited participation in the development and subsequent ownership of the Acholi version (See C. Burke and D.N. Kobusingiye, 2014, p. 44); 2) The question of whether customary law should be codified at all, since customary rules by their very nature are not a static set of rules. See for a discussion on this topic in the context of Acholi e.g. J. Hopwood and R.R. Atkinson, 2013, pp. 4–5.

163 J. Hopwood, 2015, p. 394.

island in order to benefit from the relative wealth in comparison to Eastern Java. In Acholi on the other hand, land is still available in abundance.

A major difference regarding the customary law systems in Bali and Acholi is the way in which women's rights are affected. Although not ideal in terms of providing equal land rights, the Acholi customary law is largely beneficial for women because much of the land still is communal land, which is in the hands of clans. The predominantly male stewards have the responsibility to see to it that all clan members, men and women alike, have access to land while male clan members also do not have individual ownership rights over land. This communal land concept, which is favourable for women, has all but disappeared in Bali. Furthermore, under Acholi customary law widows seem to have a strong position because in principle they take the place of their deceased husband as head of the household.

Since under customary law Balinese Hindu women are denied inheritance rights – the most likely way for a person to gain property rights over land – the customary rules are disadvantageous. Widows may still have access to their deceased husband's family land, but this depends on the goodwill of their in-laws or their son(s).

As regards access to remedies under the customary settlement systems, it appears that the Acholi system offers real opportunities for women to effectuate their rights provided that she is a member of a strong clan. The Adat law remedies in Bali, however, seem to be ineffective for women since these will apply traditional rules that deny women property rights over land.

7.2. SIMILARITIES

Both States have ratified the UN human rights conventions that are relevant in this context. In addition, Uganda is also a party to the African Charter on Human and Peoples' Rights and the Maputo Protocol in which women's right to equality is reaffirmed. Moreover, both States have a Constitution that guarantees equality and non-discrimination for all individuals and both have adopted legislation and have created organs that further women's rights. Irrespective of these positive developments, in both States discriminatory national legislation can still be found. Such legislation will be based on the stereotypical notion that men and women play different societal roles and that a man is the head of the family with all ensuing benefits such as preference in relation to land titling and preferential treatment as regards the inheritance.

In both cases there are ambiguities and misunderstandings with regard to the relationship between the customary and the national legal system. Also, as far as international human rights obligations are concerned, it appears that in both countries insufficient attention has been paid to the implementation of the rights contained in the respective treaties. Moreover, local legislative, executive, and judiciary are generally not well enough informed about these international rights and may be under the impression that the ensuing obligations are not relevant to the customary system. Since both States explicitly allow personal status laws and traditions for ethnic or religious groups, the result is that the land rights of Acholi and Balinese women are not in conformity with the international norms that have been agreed upon by the respective States.

In both situations we find traditional, patriarchal societies where women and men have complementary rather than equal roles. The situation is better described by the term 'equity' than 'equality',[164] and women enjoy the privilege to access land of their family, in-laws or community instead of having secure and autonomous property rights over land. Though the situation of Acholi women may be better in comparison to that of Balinese women, still they have fewer rights than men. Both for Acholi and Balinese women tradition and cultural identity is of great importance. Women want to fit in with their clan or community because it gives them a sense of security and belonging. The women depend on their clan or family members as their safety net and social relations. That is why they wish to uphold customary rules and traditions even if they are aware of the fact that these are not always to their advantage.

In general, in both regions access to remedies under the formal judiciary system is difficult for women. Making use of the formal dispute settlement system is not acceptable because it deviates from the idea that disputes should be settled in harmony within the traditional societal structure, restoring the balance within the community. Furthermore, accessing official remedies is expensive and may include other barriers such as long distances and corruption.

Below, the two tables that were used earlier to illustrate the land rights situation of different categories of women according to marital status within the Balinese and Acholi contexts separately have been merged into one table. It becomes apparent that the similarities are striking. The only difference concerns the situation where a woman is a widow. Under Balinese Adat law this woman has access to her son's or her in-laws' land. Under Acholi customary law, the woman may choose between access to her late husband's or her blood relatives' land. It should be borne in mind, however, that in practice, an Acholi widow may meet with resistance when

164 The term equity is understood as what is regarded to be 'fair' in a certain context. If it is accepted as a given fact that men and women play different roles in society, it is seen as fair that the male breadwinner will earn a higher income and is entitled to receive a greater share of the inheritance since he is supposed to provide for his family. Also see H. Charlesworth, and C. Chinkin, *The boundaries of international law; A feminist analysis*, Manchester University Press, Manchester 2000, p. 80.

she wants to stay on her in-law's land or when she reclaims her right to her blood relatives' land.

Category of person	**Access to their blood relatives' land**	**Access to their husband's family's land**
Unmarried woman	● ◆	
Married woman		● ◆
Widow	●	● ◆
Divorced woman	● ◆	

Acholi= ● / Balinese = ◆

In conclusion it can be stated that customary laws and practices concerning property rights over land tend to disadvantage women because they are based on patriarchy and stereotypes with the result that women may enjoy privileges concerning access to land, but are denied secure and autonomous property rights over land. The majority of girls and women in both cases are economically dependent, which puts them in a vulnerable and insecure position.

7.3. POSSIBLE SOLUTIONS

While the form of property right of land is not all-determinant – although of course ownership rights trump access rights – what is most important for women is security of tenure; the certainty that she will have a place to live and that land rights are guaranteed irrespective of location or status in society. The knowledge that a woman who works on the land will continue to have access to the same plot of land and that she can decide what is going to happen with the harvest and the proceeds, will induce her to spend more time and energy on the land and maybe to invest in new agricultural techniques. This will not only benefit herself and her family, but it is also expected that if women have secure property rights over land on any significant scale it will increase agricultural productivity, which is of particular importance to developing States.[165] For this reason, both legal and other appropriate measures should be taken to increase security of tenure for women.

From the two cases it has become clear that national and local laws are discriminatory and thus are in violation with international standards. Legislators at the central and at the local level have the obligation to bring all laws in conformity with the basic human rights principles of equality and non-discrimination. This may entail that personal status rules have to be overturned. While the law may

165 B. Agarwal, *A Field of One's Own; Gender and Land Rights in South Asia*, Cambridge University Press 1994, pp. 33–34.

not be the designated tool to change society, in any case, equality before the law will mean a secure basis and something women can fall back on to claim their rights.

Changing the laws will have to go hand in hand with training the judiciary, as well as law enforcers, local councils, mediators, and community or clan leaders in order to guarantee that human rights obligations are understood and are implemented in a uniform way. It is important that irrespective of the location or the community, legal security is created.

Access to remedies remains a problem since the local councils that are easily approached by women may be biased and stuck in traditional ways. Both States should take measures to guarantee that review of local decisions becomes easy and virtually free of costs so that women who are deprived of their rights do not have to incur high costs and travel long distances in order to appeal to a more neutral court. A solution for some women may be creating 'mobile' courts that visit rural areas on a regular basis instead of women having to go to unknown far-away cities.

Both States have influential land acts that could be used to bring about a change for the better for women. In Acholi it is probably best that the traditional system of communal land – which is quite beneficial for women – is maintained, but secure access should be improved. Progress could for instance be achieved by revising the formal law where relevant. A reference in the Land Act of Uganda to the 'head of household' as the person representing a family for the purpose of holding land under customary tenure disadvantages women, since generally men are seen as heads of household. This is therefore an example of a provision that should be altered. Progress could also be achieved by responding to the needs of those local leaders in charge of seeing to the application of Acholi customary law. This might take the form of dialogue on how to address certain challenges or sensitisation on the equal rights of women.[166] It might also just entail the provision of logistical support.

In Bali, it may be too difficult to turn back time and reintroduce communal land with every village. However, where communal land is still in existence, it should be made accessible to the landless with security of tenure giving priority to unmarried, divorced, and widowed women.

In both States the position of female farmers must be strengthened. They should be acknowledged as independent farmers both before the law and in practice. Authorities and communities must be convinced of the fact that a lack of property rights or decision-making powers of female farmers will lead to the loss of productivity.

Institutions for the effective management of land should be established or strengthened where they are already in place.

166 J. Hopwood, 2015, p. 409.

As far as extra-legal measures are concerned, it seems imperative that the authorities deploy the services of societal actors that have the possibility to bring about a change of mentality without harming the core cultural values of a community or clan.

It will depend on the circumstances of the case and the susceptibility for change of the community which actors may have the best chance to influence people's mind sets. In Uganda, international CSOs/NGOs may be accepted to inform and educate the population, while in Bali it became clear that international interference may be refused and that even local NGOs cannot accept financial support from international sources since this would disqualify them in the eyes of the local population. In both cases, local grass roots organizations may have the best papers to inform and educate and persuade the local authorities that things should change. It is the governments' obligation to support these CSOs financially.

It goes without saying that change can hardly happen without the support of religious and community leaders. If they can be convinced that the cultural identity of their community can be preserved when women get equal access and property rights over land, customary laws and traditions may be changed. In addition to CSO representatives, they may listen to hitherto unexpected actors like the Balinese academics who are eminently suited to influence the mentality of their original communities.

In any case, use should be made of the dynamic character of culture since change will unavoidably come in the long run. Whether that will be a change for the better will depend on strategic choices that are being made since investing in cultural expressions that have the greatest impact on a certain society may pay off in the end. Television and radio programmes may have a useful impact, but also new popular stories, plays and songs may persuade people to discard old ideas and embrace new traditions based on gender equality. Sociologists and cultural anthropologists are better suited than lawyers to advise the authorities what will work in this respect.

8. CONCLUDING REMARKS

States that are parties to human rights treaties and at the same time want to accommodate traditional, ethnic, or religious communities have to make certain that personal laws are brought in conformity with the international obligations in respect of equal access to and property rights over land for men and women.

Customary laws and traditions are not necessarily to women's detriment; where they procure equal rights for women, efforts should be made to maintain them. However, customs that discriminate against women should be modified in such a way that change is acceptable to the community and will not disrupt a community's cultural identity.

Property rights over land can take many forms and all of them may be beneficial for women if they go hand in hand with the certainty that they can be enjoyed as long as needed. That is why security of tenure is the key issue that should be achieved irrespective of location or marital status of the women involved.

While it is clear that the authorities have important obligations, they have to recruit the help of non-State actors to actually change the population's mentality since real change can only happen from the inside. Instrumental in this regard may be the age-old cultural expressions that have a huge impact on the way a community thinks and acts. Harmful traditions can be replaced by beneficial ones if the right tools are put in the hands of the most suitable actors.

AGRARIAN REFORM AND SMALLHOLDER RIGHTS IN INDONESIA: ALTERNATIVES TO CORPORATE, CUSTOMARY AND PRIVATE OWNERSHIP

Ben White

1. INDONESIAN LAND RIGHTS: VISION AND REALITY

Indonesian land laws and regulations, as in many other countries, provide a fine vision of egalitarian, prosperous smallholder farmer communities, producing food and other crops on sustainable farms with secure tenure. But this contrasts sharply with the situation existing on the ground. In this chapter I will raise the question: what kinds of land tenure regimes are needed in Indonesia and similar countries, to promote just and equitable access to land for those who need it, and who can make good use of it for the benefit of themselves and society?

The Indonesian Constitution and basic land laws, developed in the early years of independence, are quite clear about the need for land to have a 'social function' and to be used for the 'greatest possible prosperity of the people'. We find for example, in the Indonesian Constitution: 'The earth, water and natural resources contained in them are controlled by the State and [are to be] used for the greatest possible prosperity of the people',[1] and in the Basic Agrarian Law of 1960: 'The State's right of control gives it the authority [...] to determine and regulate the legal relations between people and earth, water and atmosphere', and 'All rights to land [should] have a social function'.[2]

In recent years new laws on food, on protection of agricultural land and on the protection and empowerment of farmers have given further shape to this vision, including the obligation of the State to guarantee security of tenure, to provide

1 Constitution of the Republic of Indonesia, Section XIV, Article 33(3). All translations from Indonesian language are by the author.

2 Basic Agrarian Law 1960, Articles 2 and 6.

land to those smallholder farmers who need it, and to increase employment opportunities in agriculture, underlining consistently that the regulation of land tenure, food production and support to farmers must be based on principles of 'cooperation, equality, sustainability, and justice', and with special priority for small farmers:

> The organization of food production will be based on the principles of sovereignty, self-sufficiency, security, safety, utility, equality, sustainability and justice.[3]

> The National and Regional Governments have the obligation to provide a guarantee of provision of agricultural land [by] facilitating access to state land [...] providing loans to farmers empowering them to obtain agricultural land [... and] providing rights to leasehold and use-rights [and in all these activities giving] priority to farmers who own less than 2.0 hectares of farmland, and landless farmers who cultivate less than 2.0 hectares.[4]

These beautiful visions of regimes of land rights serving a social function for the greatest possible prosperity of the people, are echoed in the visions of agrarian social movements. Indonesia's *Federasi Serikat Petani Indonesia* (Federation of Indonesian Peasants' Unions, whose slogan on their logo is 'land to the tiller!') proclaims a vision of 'agrarian renewal' for the maximum welfare of rural people:

> Agrarian renewal is a corrective effort to reform the unequal agrarian structure which makes exploitation possible towards a new structure rooted in agrarian justice, [that is] a situation which guarantees there will be no concentration of control of agrarian resources in the hands of the few. [...] to create a process of change and re-structuring of rural society, to create a basis for healthy, modern agriculture, security of land tenure as the source of people's livelihoods, a system of social welfare and social security for rural people, and the use of natural resources for the maximum possible prosperity of the people.[5]

But all these beautiful visions stand in contrast to the realities of land control in Indonesia (as in many other countries) today.

In many regions of Indonesia, smallholder farmers cultivate their land under conditions of insecure tenure, making them vulnerable to dispossession. Large-scale land concessions to powerful agribusiness companies are often the subject

---

3 Law no. 18 of 2012 on Food.

4 Law no. 19 of 2013 on Protection and Empowerment of Farmers.

5 Federasi Serikat Petani Indonesia, 'Pandangan dan sikap dasar Federasi Serikat Petani Indonesia (FPSI) terhadap pembaruan agraria' 2003, Lawang, para's C1, 2 and 4. www.spi.or.id/wpcontent/uploads/2008/08/pembaruanagraria.pdf, accessed 28 October 2014. I also looked for an agrarian vision, but did not find one, on the two competing web-sites of the more official All-Indonesia Farmer's Harmony Association HKTI, a relic of the Suharto period (hkti.or.id and hkti.org).

of deals made over the heads of local smallholders (particularly outside Java). In other regions where individual property titles are well established, we find quite seriously distorted patterns of ownership, with growing inequality of holdings in areas of small-scale private commercial or semi-commercial farming (as in Java); in many regions the majority of rural households now are completely landless, or operate small farms as share tenants on terms that are very disadvantageous. This situation is worsened when fertile irrigated land becomes an attractive object of speculation and accumulation in the hands of absentee owners, leading to rapidly rising land prices as we see in many regions.

Smallholder farming is under pressure, in Indonesia and all over the world. Maybe this is one reason why the year 2014 was designated by the United Nations as the 'International Year of the Family Farm'. Though some international organizations (like FAO, IFAD, ILC) took it seriously and embarked on programmes of policy research and publicity campaigns, the year seems to have passed without attracting much notice or having much impact among UN Member States. Still, this makes it an appropriate time for us to think about the future of 'family' or 'smallholder' farming in Indonesia and in different parts of the world.

What kinds of farms, a generation from now, will provide Indonesia's growing population with its needs for food and other agricultural products? Will they be 'smallholdings' – held by individuals rather than corporations, and managed by people who also work on them, with or without some hired help? Or will we see an increasing dominance of large-scale, corporate, heavily mechanized agriculture? Behind this question lies an ongoing global 'battle for agriculture' between large-scale, industrial, energy intensive, earth-warming, water-wasting, unsustainable forms of agricultural production on the one hand, and on the other a hard-pressed small-farm alternative which claims to be able both to feed the world, to do this in sustainable ways, and also to provide employment and incomes to vastly greater numbers of people than industrial farming. The coming years will see how this battle is resolved.

If we do promote the idea of smallholder farming, will the next generation of young men and women wishing to become farmers have any realistic chance of getting hold of a piece of land to farm, while they are still young? What sorts of institutions do they need to support them? And in particular, what forms and principles of land tenure support smallholder farming, and the creation or strengthening of relatively egalitarian communities of prosperous, small-scale farmers? What form(s) of tenure give smallholders secure land rights, and maintain (relatively) egalitarian agrarian structures, and at the same time give women and young would-be farmers access to land? And when local communities are given authority to allocate land rights (as I think they should be), how can local people be protected, when necessary, from misbehaviour of their own elites?

In thinking about these questions it is useful first, to recall some peculiar characteristics of land compared to other resources and goods.[6] Land is extremely heterogeneous in nature and quality. Control over land is indispensable to almost all human activity, and people have strong attachments to it (whether to a family farm, their neighbourhood or village, or their ethnic/political territory). Land does not move and therefore cannot be exported, and 'it is not consumed through use in the way that other resources are' and therefore is commonly rented, or allocated in the form of use-rights (while it is unlikely that anyone would want, for example, to borrow or rent 12 tons of iron ore).

Finally and most importantly, land is an 'excludable' resource: it is possible to prevent others from having access to it, whether through regulation, force, or – when land becomes a commodity which can be freely bought and sold – through the market. 'Exclusion' is thus, a necessary feature of every type of land use and tenurial arrangement. The laws and regulations (whether formal or customary) which provide exclusive access for some come into tension with the fact that others cannot access it, even though their need for it may be as great, or greater.[7] This is why we need States to make rules governing access to and exclusion from land, and to do this in such a way that land has, and keeps, its 'social function'.

In the rest of this chapter I will argue that we need to think of alternatives to what are currently the three dominant forms of land tenure – private individual land ownership, customary tenure, and large-scale land concessions – since all these are part of the problem rather than of the solution. The focus is on Indonesia but in some places I will make reference to other countries.

2. LAND PROBLEMS IN INDONESIA: LEGACIES OF THE COLONIAL AND RECENT PAST

Indonesia has a difficult and in some periods tragic history of land policy and land reform. Colonial distortions have never been fully corrected and in some cases were strengthened or even worsened by subsequent law-making. One important example is the 1967 and 1999 Forest Laws, which declared some 65 per cent of Indonesia's land mass to be State-owned forest land and therefore under the control of the Ministry of Forestry. Cultivators in these vast expanses of 'political forest' (which in many cases are not forest at all) are chronically liable to dispossession and to land deals which are often made without even consulting

6 These points are taken, with some additions, from D. Hall, *Land*, Polity Press, Cambridge 2013, pp. 6–10.

7 D. Hall, P. Hirsch and T. Murray Li, *Powers of Exclusion: Land Dilemmas in Southeast Asia*, NUS Press, Singapore 2011, NUS Press, Ch. 1.

them.[8] Partly resulting from these laws, and the failure to implement the Basic Agrarian Law of 1960 (perhaps we should say, the failure to implement and update this half-century old law), we see many persistent problems of land conflicts and inequalities in access to land, some of which I have already mentioned briefly.

The land and tenancy reform laws passed in 1960 basically reproduced the standard non-socialist model of land reform, based on principles of private ownership, maximum and minimum holdings limits, and conversion of tenancy into ownership rights. Reforms on this model had been applied successfully with US backing in Japan, South Korea and Taiwan, and many other countries tried to replicate these reforms with Western support but with varying degrees of success.[9] The new laws were originally opposed by the Indonesian Communist Party (PKI) and its affiliate the Indonesian Peasants' Front (BTI) since they were based on private ownership. Once they had been passed, however, the PKI and BTI campaigned at local level for the implementation of these (anti-communist) reforms, making enemies among the landed rural elites, and that was one main reason why they became the victims of the anti-communist purges and massacres of 1965–66.[10]

Agrarian reform implementation was abandoned and became a taboo subject for many years post-1966. The popular 'mass guidance' programmes of the BTI and university students which had tried to help peasants increase production were replaced with the disastrous *Bimas Gotong Royong* programme, in which the new regime contracted with multinational corporations for provision of the new 'Green Revolution' inputs including fertilizers, insecticides, extension and management, and the new IR paddy varieties which had become available from Los Banos. The corporations were allocated huge areas of rice fields (often around 50,000 ha) and were paid around US$50 per ha for providing the inputs and management, and peasants were expected to repay these inputs by delivering one-sixth of their crop to a national collecting agency. Mismanagement and corruption made a near disaster of this programme, which was abruptly terminated in 1970 when the State took direct control of the *Bimas* and *Inmas* programmes, recognizing the crucial importance of food production and stable food prices for political stability.[11]

---

8 N.L. Peluso, *Rich Forests, Poor People*, University of California Press, Berkeley 1992; M.A. Safitri, *Forest Tenure in Indonesia: The Socio-Legal Challenges of Securing Communities' Rights*. Dissertation, Leiden University 2010.

9 D. Christodoulou, *The Unpromised Land: Agrarian reform and Conflict Worldwide*, London, Zed Books 1990; M. Lipton, *Land Reform in Developing Countries: Property Rights and Property Wrongs*, London, Routledge 2010.

10 R. Cribb (ed.), *The Indonesian Killings of 1965–66. Studies from Java and Bali*. Clayton, Monash University Papers on Southeast Asia No. 21, 1990; D. Kammen & K. McGregor (eds), *The Contours of Mass Violence in Indonesia, 1965–68*. Singapore, NUS Press and NIAS Press 2012.

11 F. Hüsken and B. White, 'Java: social differentiation, food production and agrarian control', in G. Hart, A. Turton and B. White (eds) *Agrarian Transformations: Local Processes and the*

One important consequence for smallholder land rights has been the complete absence, since 1965, of any democratic national peasant movement defending smallholder interests and rights. The BTI (which claimed 6 million members) and all other peasant organizations were dissolved and replaced in the beginning of the 1970s with a single, State-sponsored monolith organization, the 'Indoncsia Farmers' Harmony Association' (HKTI). This organization has not supported efforts of small-scale farmers to hold on to their land in the face of State or corporate land grabbing. In recent years for example HKTI has been completely silent in the face of the massive forced expulsion of local peasants from millions of hectares of land for corporate agriculture (especially oil palm). The HKTI has for some years been locked in a leadership struggle. In 2004, Suharto's former son-in-law Prabowo Subianto managed to be elected as head of the HKTI, and sought re-appointment at the HKTI National Assembly in 2010, hoping thus to be in a good position to garner the 'peasant vote' as candidate for President in the 2014 elections. Although Prabowo financed the entire event, hosting hundreds of delegates in an expensive resort hotel in Bali, competing candidates claimed that his re-appointment was not valid and set up a rival HKTI assembly and structure, electing as their own leader the businessman Oesman Sapta Odang.[12] The two rival HKTIs continue to claim legitimacy, and as can be seen from their two competing web sites, neither has any vision of agrarian renewal.[13] The losers are the peasants and farm workers whose interests the HKTI is formally mandated to defend.

Meanwhile, various smaller peasant and indigenous people's organizations which have emerged since the fall of Suharto have campaigned for a revival of agrarian reform efforts, and new law making. In 2013 the Constitutional Court reached a historic decision, in a case brought by the Alliance of Customary Communities of the Indonesian Archipelago (AMAN), that 'customary forest' zones (*hutan adat*) are not State property under the authority of the Ministry of Forestry, but part of 'adat zones' and the property of customary communities (*masyarakat hukum adat*).[14] In recent years, two attempts at new agrarian law-making, one on land rights generally and the other on rights of customary law communities (*Masyarakat Hukum Adat*), have encountered problems in their progress to

State in Southeast Asia, Berkeley: University of California Press 1989, pp. 251–2. *Bimas* = mass giuidance, *Inmas* = mass intensifcation, *gotong royong* = (lit.) shouldering the burden together.

12 www.tempo.co/read/news/2010/07/13/078263172/Munas-HKTI-Kisruh-Muncul-Desakan-Forum-Tandingan, accessed 17 January 2015, and various related news items on the same site.

13 Hkti.or.id and hkti.org.

14 For the full text of the decision and a comprehensive introduction and commentary, see Noer Fauzi Rachman and Mia Siscawati, *Masyarakat Hukum Adat adalah Pemnyandang Hak, Subjek Hukum, dan Pemilik Wilayah Adatnya: Memahami secara Kontekstual Putusan Mahkamah Konstitusi Replublik Indonesia atas Perkara Nomor 35/PU-X/2012*, Jogjakarta, INSIST Press 2014.

adoption.[15] Even if adopted, however, these two draft laws would have done little if anything to address many of the problems I have raised.

3. WHY PRIORITIZE SMALLHOLDER FARMING?

First, we need to establish the case for the support of smallholder farming (as opposed to large-scale, corporate plantations, food estates etc.). We need to do this because of the strength of the idea, common among policymakers, technocrats, agricultural economists and the business community generally, that modern, efficient, innovative agriculture requires a shift from smaller- to larger-scale farming, from family agriculture to corporate farming.

Large-scale, government-supported corporate acquisition of contested lands and common lands, and the accompanying dispossession of local farmers, and forest users is currently occurring on an unprecedented scale. These deals are usually accompanied by government and corporate promises to develop modern, industrial forms of agricultural production for export, and to provide good jobs and incomes for local people. But research has long ago shown that these industrial (capital- and energy-intensive) forms of agriculture are unsustainable. They also do not provide employment on any significant scale, tending to create enclaves of capital intensive, monocrop farming with minimal linkages to the local economy.[16] In Indonesia, every attempt to develop large-scale rice estates outside Java, in the colonial period, in the Suharto period, and in the last few years, has failed and it is surprising to see ambitious new plans for such estates in such places as Merauke and Kalimantan.

In fact, there is no agricultural crop which cannot be grown efficiently and effectively on smallholdings and in general the smaller the farm size, the higher the productivity per hectare.[17] This includes both food crops and the major export

---

[15] In September 2014 the Draft Law on Land was withdrawn by the government from its process through the Parliament (www.hukumonline.com/berita/baca/lt542a3f109fbbe/ruu-pertanahan-dan-ruu-tapera-gagal-jadi-uu) Although the relevant Parliamentary Committee planned to complete a new version and see it through Parliament by the end of 2015, at the tie of writing (February 2016) there was no indication of progress. The government's draft Law on Recognition and Protection of the Rights of Adat Law Communities, www.djpp.kemenkumham.go.id/pembahasan-ruu/63-rancangan-peraturan-pemerintah/2453-rancangan-undang-undang-tentang-pengakuan-dan-perlindungan-hak-masyarakat-hukum-adat.html was contested by AMAN, who have campaigned for adoption of many changes in the text, and progress on this law also appears to have come to a halt www.aman.or.id/wp-content/plugins/downloads-manager/upload/RUU PPHMA versi AMAN.pdf. All sites accessed on 9 February 2016.

[16] The classic statement on the link between enclave plantation economy and persistent rural poverty is G.L. Beckford, *Persistent Poverty: Underdevelopment in the Plantation Economies of the Third World*, London, Zed Books 1972.

[17] B. White, 'Does Indonesia need corporate farming? Reflections on modernization, efficiency and the social function of land, *Journal of Rural Indonesia* I no. 1, 2014, http://ejournal.skpm.

crops. Just look for example at the tiny rice farms of Java and Bali, averaging less than half a hectare and often as small as one-fifth of a hectare. They routinely achieve average yields of 6–7 tons per ha, twice a year, and in some case 8, 9 and 10 tons; while the newly opened rice estates in Ketapang, West Kalimantan, despite all the support in terms of expertise and equipment given to them by many different BUMNs following Presidential Instruction, so far have difficulty achieving yields of even 2 tons per hectare.

It is not only peasant movements and romantics who argue that smallholder farming can feed the world. Despite continuous assaults on their lands, and on their rights to farm, small-scale producers continue to be the world's, and Indonesia's majority food producers. There is a growing scientific consensus on the potentials for high-productivity, resilient smallholder farming using non-industrial and agro-ecological practices, if adequately supported.[18] There are of course economies of scale in the agricultural sector, but they are generally not to be found on the farm itself. Economies of scale are needed, and realized, not on the farm but in some of the activities upstream and downstream from farms in domestic or global agricultural commodity chains: the production and provision of the necessary physical and non-physical inputs (including not only equipment but also some kinds of knowledge), and the processing, storage and marketing of the crop.

There is also something to be learned from history here. Historically, many powerful regimes have allowed, encouraged or themselves engineered the emergence of large-scale landholdings (from ancient Egypt and the Roman Empire to European colonial plantations and Soviet or Chinese collectivization). But in all these cases, subsequent regimes have opted for economic development and social peace by breaking down these holdings in favour of more efficient smallholder farming.[19] The World Bank was one important actor in these changes in the 1970s and 1980s, including in Indonesia.

There are many other advantages to smallholder farming in terms of Indonesia's developmental goals. It is not possible to go into details here, but one key development priority for Indonesia is the provision of employment. Smallholder

---

ipb.ac.id/index.php/ruralindonesia; J.-D. van der Ploeg, *The New Peasantries: Struggles for Autonomy and Sustainability in an Era of Empire and Globalization*. London, Earthscan 2008.

18 P. McMichael, 'A comment on Henry Bernstein's way with peasants, and food sovereignty', *The Journal of Peasant Studies*, 2014, http://dx.doi.org/10.1080/03066150.2014.936853, pp. 4–5. IAASTD, *International Assessment of Agricultural Knowledge, Science and Technology for Development: Synthesis Report*. Washington DC: Island Press 2008; Committee on Food Security, *Investing in smallholder agriculture for food security. Report of the High Level Panel of Experts on Food Security and Nutrition*. Rome, Committee on Food Security 2013.

19 M. Mazoyer and L. Roudart, *A History of World Agriculture from the Neolithic Time to the Present*, New York, Monthly Review Press 2014.

farming has a much higher labour absorption rate than large-scale industrial farming.

The former UN Special Rapporteur on the Right to Food, Olivier De Schutter has been a lone voice within the UN family arguing for a broader vision: not to deny the need for investment in agriculture, but to develop an alternative programme for agricultural investment based on reorientation of agricultural systems towards modes of production that are both productive and sustainable. De Schutter therefore argues:

> 'Land investments implying an important shift in land rights should represent *the last and least desirable option*, acceptable only if no other investment model can achieve a similar contribution to local development.'[20]

4. PROBLEMS OF 'CUSTOMARY' AND PRIVATE OWNERSHIP

Let us suppose then, that we are interested in promoting land tenure regimes that support and promote smallholder production, because this is good for employment, equality, environment, productivity, and social justice. This means, among other things, that smallholders must have security of tenure. While land laws and peasant movements agree on this principle, it is not always clear exactly what kind of land tenure regimes land reforms and peasant movements actually want (in terms of concrete tenure systems).

What kind or kinds of land tenure regimes, then, are most appropriate? Most policy thinking, and the thinking of most agrarian movements, points in two directions: first, individual private property rights, and second, in certain regions, recognition of customary or communal rights. In Indonesia, as already noted, two new land laws are in preparation, one on the recognition and protection of customary communities (and their rights to land and territory) and the other a general land law, covering five different forms of land rights and including a detailed section on individual ownership rights.[21]

---

20 UN General Assembly, *Report submitted by the Special Rapporteur on the Right to Food.* New York, United Nations General Assembly, Human Rights Council, 16th session, December 2010, p. 20, emphasis added; also O. de Schutter, 'How not to think of land-grabbing : three critiques of large-scale investments in farmland', *The Journal of Peasant Studies* 38(2), 2012, pp. 249–79.

21 See note 14.

4.1. PROBLEMS OF 'CUSTOMARY RIGHTS' IN LAND

'Customary rights to land' (of the kind that will be recognized in new laws-in-the-making) have many problems, even if recognized by the State and protected in law. This is a sensitive issue, difficult to discuss. The basic idea of 'customary rights' ('indigenous people's rights') in fact, runs counter to the basic principles of most land reforms. The question of who qualifies as 'indigenous people' or 'customary' society is complex, unresolved, and highly political. Indeed, the whole idea that land rights should be allocated on the basis of a person's identity, rather than his or her need or capacity to use the land, is highly controversial

> 'From the perspective of indigeneity and ethno-territory, only the people with ancestral claims to land have the right to determine who should have access and who should be excluded, [while] from the perspective of land reform ... the key to a just distribution is the need for land as the basis of an agrarian livelihood.'[22]

Besides that, however, there are also huge areas of Indonesia's so-called forest lands where non-indigenous communities, or communities of mixed indigenous and incomer ethnicity, have been allocating use-rights among themselves for decades but do not claim the status of *masyarakat adat*, and thus would be excluded from the provisions of laws based on indigenous or *adat* status.

As Daniel Fitzpatrick recently observed:

> 'Many land relations in modern Indonesia do not fit easily into the binary classification of 'state titles' and 'adat rights' [...] In fact they exist in a world of legal and normative uncertainty, uncertain licences to occupy revocable at the discretion of an often corrupt and rapacious elite.'[23]

The unjust and insecure tenure situation of many informal and semi-formal land occupiers in Indonesia was not resolved by the Basic Agrarian Law (BAL) of 1960, and is not changed in any substantive way by subsequent draft laws on agrarian resources,[24] or as far as I can see by the two new land laws in preparation.

There are various additional problems with 'customary tenure'. When use-rights are allocated by customary leaders (nearly always, elderly men) they do not provide adequately for the needs and rights of either women or young people who may need land as the basis for a livelihood. There has also been a tendency, in the

---

22 Hall, Hirsch and Li, *Powers of Exclusion*, p. 183.

23 D. Fitzpatrick, 'Land, custom and the state in post-Suharto Indonesia: a lawyer's perspective', in J.S. Davidson and D. Henley (eds.), *The Revival of Tradition in Indonesian Politics: The Deployment of adat from Colonialism to Indigenism*. London, Routledge Contemporary Southeast Asia Series 2007, p. 131.

24 Fitzpatrick, 'Land, custom and the state', pp. 139, 143.

current era of corporate land acquisition, for *adat* leaders to enrich themselves and their cronies by facilitating land deals which may erode or completely destroy smallholder customary rights. As one Indonesian speaker remarked, at an international conference in Bali some years ago: 'what Indonesia's indigenous people need most of all today, is protection from their own elites'. I will come back to these questions later.

4.2. PROBLEMS OF PRIVATE INDIVIDUAL TITLING: THE DE SOTO FALLACY

The other main thrust of agrarian laws and policies in Indonesia and many other countries, as the answer to tenurial and transactional land insecurity, has been the focus on top-down individual land titling programmes, creating individual private property in land.[25] These appear to be given some prominence in the new Land Law currently in preparation.

Land titling, unlike customary tenure, gives the individual owner a 'complete bundle of rights' – 'the right to exclusive use of a parcel of land, irrespective of the social identity of the owner'.[26] Behind this trend lies a general (but historically inaccurate) idea that land rights move inevitably, and universally, in the direction of private property. This 'evolutionary theory of land rights' sees private land titling as the natural end point of land rights formalization – the point at which the process is 'finished'. Land titling is seen by its proponents as inclusive, democratic and pro-poor; it is the key element in the vision of the Peruvian economist Hernando de Soto, who argues that it is the way to include the poor in the modern economy.[27] While the globalization of individual property rights has indeed been a general trend, there is nothing inevitable about it; it has been the result of State policies, often but not always influenced by international agencies and bilateral donors, and can as easily be undone by State policies.[28]

As we can see in the abundant, empirically-based critiques of De Soto and other proponents of the evolutionary theory, individual land titling brings with it many problems. This is a difficult and often sensitive question, since smallholders with insecure tenure often dream of getting ownership titles. But there are so many examples of cases where titles have been distributed and within a few years many of the new title holders have already lost their land, due either to the chronic

25 Fitzpatrick, 'Land, custom and the state', p. 144.
26 Hall, Hirsch and Li, *Powers of Exclusion*, p. 36.
27 H. de Soto, *The Mystery of Capital*, New York, Basic Books 2000.
28 Hall, *Land*, p. 17; J.-P. Platteau,'The evolutionary theory of land rights as applied to Sub-Saharan Africa: a critical assessment', *Development and Change* 27, 1996, pp. 29–86.

pressures of internal differentiation that come with commercial agriculture, and/or to predatory outsiders taking advantage of the emerging land market.[29]

Land titling programmes recognize and formalize existing inequalities in land, and in this process tend to increase these inequalities. Titling does not protect the owner against loss of land rights, as many cases have shown. Even when land titles are distributed in relatively equal portions as a result of land reforms or large-scale contract-farming schemes, the beneficiary communities are subject to the chronic, built in tendencies of smallholder farmer communities to differentiate when they are involved in commercial farming, into emerging classes of landlords and larger, proto-capitalist farmers, peasant smallholders, near-landless peasants and landless workers. By making it easier both to sell land and to use it as collateral on loans, poor people become more vulnerable to dispossession through chronic debt. It increases the market value of land, leads to increases in the speculative purchase of land (by those who do not want to use it as farmers, but simply to earn income from rent and from its rising value), and thus puts acquisition of land out of reach of smallholders and younger generations

If I could mention just one documented Indonesian case of post-re-distribution land loss: Martua Sirait (researcher at ICRAF) has studied two cases of land distribution in West Java and Lampung provinces in which local peasant cultivators, after a long struggle, succeeded in having their lands converted from Forestry to the National Land Board (BPN) jurisdiction and land certificates distributed. Less than 10 years after redistribution, many title holders had lost part or all of their land, and a minority of large landholders was emerging (either from within, or through purchases by absentees). The kinds of agrarian societies emerging from this process were quite different from the egalitarian smallholder farmer societies imagined by the peasant organizations which had fought for conversion of their land to private property.[30]

Finally, land titling tends to vest titles in the 'household head', a role which is most often male (and in some parts of Southeast Asia, legally defined as male). In this process, whatever rights in land women may have had are eroded and sometimes completely destroyed. This is a commonly observed problem in redistributive land reforms,[31] and in large-scale contract-farming ventures such as oil palm in

---

29 T.A. Benjaminsen, S. Holden, C. Lund and E. Sjaastad, 'Formalisation of land rights: some empirical evidence from Mali, Niger and South Africa', *Land Use Policy* 28(1), 2009, pp. 28–35; K. Jansen and E. Roquas, 'Modernizing insecurity: the land titling project in Honduras', *Development and Change* 18(1), 1998, pp. 81–106.

30 M.T. Sirait, *Inclusion, exclusion and agrarian change: experiences in forest land redistribution in Indonesia*. PhD thesis, The Hague, International Institute of Social Studies, November 2015.

31 S. Jacobs, *Gender and Agrarian Reforms*, London, Routledge 2010.

West Kalimantan.[32] It also makes it impossible for communities to allocate use rights to the younger generation of would-be farmers, both male and female, who now have to wait until their parents die or become too elderly to use the land before taking over the parental land. Who wants to hang around in the village, waiting until they are 40 or 50 years old to become a farmer?[33] It is not surprising then that so many young villagers decide to migrate.

In summary, both customary and private-property tenure systems tend to disadvantage women; both systems make it difficult for would-be farmers to acquire farmland while still young; and both tend to result in rural societies quite different from the egalitarian smallholder communities envisioned by land laws and agrarian movements. Given the problems I have sketched above, what are the alternatives?

5. CRITERIA FOR ALTERNATIVE LAND TENURE REGIMES

What should be the principle criteria for the development of alternative land tenure regimes, better suited to present and future challenges and the needs of smallholder farming communities? Everyone will have their own list of criteria; here are mine.

a. They must prioritize smallholder farming and 'land-to-the-tiller' as a general principle (though there has to be room for some exceptions, which I will come to later).
b. They must ensure that land does not become an object of speculation or accumulation.
c. They must provide the users of land, as rights holders, with secure tenure.
d. They must allow for the regulation of access rights to land in ways that are flexible and adaptable to local conditions, and to changes in these local conditions.
e. They must ensure and protect women's equal rights to land
f. They must deal with generational tensions, enabling young would-be farmers to access land while they are still young,
g. and finally, they must not require a huge national and regional bureaucracy to implement and enforce them

32 Julia and B.White, 'Gendered experiences of dispossession: oil palm expansion in a Dayak Hibun community in West Kalimantan', *The Journal of Peasant Studies* 39(3–4), 2012, pp. 995–1016.

33 B.White, 'Agriculture and the generation problem: rural youth, employment and the future of farming' *IDS Bulletin* 43(6), 2012, pp. 9–19.

Let us explore some of these criteria, and their implications for land laws and land policies, in more detail.

First, all speculative investment in landed property is unproductive investment. It inflates land prices beyond the reach of ordinary people; it generates high levels of inequalities in society and perpetuates them through inheritance.[34] This kind of inequality is bad for the economy, for social cohesion, democracy and political stability. In short, land is much too important to be left to the free market. This means that States should make efforts to limit, and where possible to eliminate, private ownership rights in land.

This may sounds very drastic and radical, but it is actually simpler and more common than it looks. Even in the current neo-liberal order, as Ha-Jun Chang reminds us, markets of all kind are based on 'deliberately designed rules and regulations that prohibit certain things from becoming objects of exchange, discourage others, and encourage still others'.[35] Historically, States have frequently withdrawn formerly legal objects of market exchange from the market, whether as individual States through national laws, or collectively in United Nations Conventions which then are supposed to be reflected in national laws. This is why, today, we can not legally own people or buy and sell them (through the abolition of slavery); we cannot own, or buy and sell, parts of people (through abolition of the trade in human organs); we are only allowed to purchase their labour time (in labour markets), and even in labour markets we are only allowed to buy certain kinds of labour time (two ILO conventions of 1973 and 1989, for example and national laws in all countries, prohibit the sale and purchase of the labour of children).

Nearly all States – including The Netherlands, Indonesia and the United States – already have withdrawn huge areas of land from the property market. If they had not done this, we would have no national parks or municipal parks. So there is nothing drastic or shocking about the idea that States should limit, and if possible eliminate, private property in land and markets in land ownership, and also – where private property persists – limit the transmission of property to children or heirs through inheritance. It is just a question of extending these principles to agricultural land. As Thomas Piketty reminds us, Durkheim had already predicted in 1893 that modern democratic society would not put up for long with the existence of inherited wealth, and would ultimately see to it that ownership of property ended at death. The persistence of inherited wealth runs counter to meritocratic worldviews in the liberal tradition.[36]

---

34 D. Harvey, *The Enigma of Capital and the Crises of Capitalism*, London, Profile Books 2011, Ch. 7.

35 H.-J. Chang, *Economics: The User's Guide*, London, Pelican Books 2014, p. 141.

36 T.Piketty, *Capital in the Twenty-First Century*. Cambridge, MA: Harvard University Press 2014, p. 422, citing Durkheim's *The Division of Labour in Society*.

Land tenure regimes should ensure and protect secure (and egalitarian) individual use-rights. These rights must be 'secure', but must also be subject to periodic re-allocation. The 'land-to-the-tiller' principle means that rights to land are in principle ceded when the user no longer wants or is able to use the land. But there is a need for some exceptions to the general principle. Where social security systems are absent or weak, limited tenancy markets can allow the elderly, the sick etc. to retain their use rights to acquire some security of income through renting them out, and temporary out-migrants may also need to rent out their land, retaining the use-right in anticipation of their return.

In practice then, all land users become a kind of leaseholder, with secure and durable use-rights, and when rents are obtained from such leasing (which need not always be the case) these rents are due to the community rather than to private owners, becoming a significant source of local community budgets rather than going into the pockets of parasitic landlords. I see no reason why the same principles should not be applied to urban land, but I will leave that issue aside.

Flexibility and adaptability to local conditions mean that all local communities – not only indigenous/*adat* communities – must be given authority, under certain conditions, to implement land laws and to make decisions on allocation of use-rights to their members, and in some cases to negotiate use-rights for outsiders (whether individuals or firms). But this must be done in transparent and democratic ways, and this is one reason why the rules under which 'customary communities' regulate land rights also need to be adjusted and democratised. And States have to provide an effective back stop, to which citizens can have recourse when local leaders and elites try to bend the rules of the game in favour of themselves or their cronies. There seems to be no provision for this in the draft law on Customary Law Communities, which states only that the 'community' (*masyarakat*) regulates land allocation and other issues; within the black box of 'community' the nature of *adat* leaders' powers, and mechanisms for community members to control these powers, are not mentioned.

There must of course be no gender distinctions in individual use-rights, or ownership rights where they exist. More than 30 years ago the UN's Convention on the Elimination of All Forms of Discrimination Against Women – now ratified by all but a few Member States – established clearly that women must '... have access to ... equal treatment in land and agrarian reform' laws and also that they must have equal rights in intra-family property transfers through inheritance.[37] The Chicago Council on Global Affairs report on girls in rural economies around the world notes correctly that girls should be seen as future farmers and major stakeholders in agriculture and natural resource management, which requires among other things 'ensuring equitable inheritance and land rights for adolescent

[37] United Nations, *Convention on the Elimination of All Forms of Discrimination Against Women* (CEDAW) 1979, Articles 14 and 16.

girls and women by supporting efforts to change and enforce relevant national and customary laws'.[38]

In a modern system of land rights, women should have exactly the same rights in land as men, without compromise, as well as the same rights to participate as full members in farmer groups, organizations, cooperatives etc., the same rights in decisions on what crops to cultivate, the same rights to access services, instruments and mechanisms, and on whether and on what terms to engage with corporate agribusiness. This means, among other things, doing away with the practice of assigning land rights (or issuing land certificates) in the name of the 'household head' (which we see frequently in the allocation of titles in BPN's land redistribution schemes, corporate contract-farming schemes, etc.).

The issue of young people and access to land is finally getting some attention internationally,[39] but not yet in Indonesia. Young people are the most important potential source of innovation, energy and creativity in developing new, environmentally responsible and highly productive farming practices. But the number of young people in the farming population is steadily decreasing as the average age of farmers increases, both in Indonesia and other countries.

I very much doubt that Indonesia or any other country will develop land laws embodying all these principles; but it is possible, and in some cases we can see it happening, to move towards them rather than away from them. In fact, if we look around at Indonesia's neighbouring countries and some further away, and if we look within Indonesia at some specific communities we can find concrete examples of each of these principles being put into practice, although perhaps there is no example of a country, or a community, that practices them all.

5.1. THE GENERAL PRINCIPLE: COLLECTIVE OWNERSHIP, INDIVIDUAL USE RIGHTS

Several countries and many agrarian movements have adopted and implemented the principle of 'collective ownership and individual use-rights'. Some years ago (in 2000) I visited the village of Giao Lac in North Viet Nam's Red River Delta. This is a very densely populated, well-irrigated region similar to many parts of central Java. In Central Java we would find typically that 40 per cent of households own no rice-fields at all, another 40 or 50 per cent have tiny farms of 0.5 ha or less

[38] C. Bertini, *Girls Grow: A Vital Force in Rural Economies*, Chicago, Chicago Council on World Affairs 2001, p. 4.

[39] UN Food and Agriculture Organization, *Youth and Agriculture: Key Challenges and Concrete Solutions*, Rome, FAO, CTA, IFAD 2014.

and a small minority, 10 per cent or less, own more than a half of all the land. In Giao Lac, in contrast, every household had secure use-rights to land.

Under government Resolution 10, which had been implemented in 1988, farmer ownership of machines, water buffalo, cattle and agricultural tools was recognized, but not ownership of the farmland itself. But for the first time since the 1960s, every single household in Giao was provided with longer-term land use rights, and more freedom of choice in deciding what to plant. These use rights were allocated using a very simple formula, as a crude standard of need. Each household received an allocation of irrigated land, based on the number of members (1.5 *sao* or 490 square metres per household member). A household of 5 persons would thus have secure rights to 5 × 1.5 × 0.0360 = 0.27 ha of irrigated rice land; a household of 4 persons, 4 × 1.5 × 0.0360 = 0.22 ha. Paddy yields were on average 6.3 tons /ha, with two harvests each year = 12.6 tons/year/ha, similar to yields in Java. These secure use rights were granted for a period of 15 years, after which they would be re-adjusted if necessary to new demographic conditions.[40]

There is no reason why local communities, empowered by national laws to manage land-use rights allocation, should not adopt similar principles of collective ownership and individual use rights, periodically redistributed. This principle in fact has a long history in Indonesian pre-colonial and colonial history, having been practiced in many parts of Central and East Java.

5.2. USING COMMUNITY-OWNED LAND TO PROVIDE USE-RIGHTS TO THE POOR, NEAR-LANDLESS, YOUNG FARMERS, ETC.

Besides 'radical' solutions through Land Reform laws, there are many possibilities at local level to shift land tenure status away from private ownership and towards collective ownership and private use rights.

In many regions of Java, quite substantial portions of farm land are already owned by the village in the form of *Tanah Bengkok, Tanah Kas Desa* or *Tanah Kemakmuran*. Use-rights to these lands, in smallholder units, are commonly allocated each year or each few years in some form of auction or lottery process and villages are allowed to determine their own ways of doing this. In some of the villages which we have studied, we have found that only the landless and the near-landless can apply.

40 1 *sao* = 360 m². Le Thi Van Hue, *Coastal Resource Use and Management in a Village of Northern Vietnam*. The Hague, International Institute of Social Studies, PhD thesis 2004, pp. 112–3, 133. For more information on Viet Nam's resolution 10, Jacobs, *Gender and Agrarian Reforms*, pp. 111–118.

There is no reason why village communities should not decide that the village has first option on purchase of private land that comes up for sale, to build up the village's collective property of *Kas Desa* land. The income from renting out these lands to smallholders then becomes a growing source of community income for the funding of development projects, rather than going into the pockets of private landowners. During the recent Presidential election campaign both candidates, if I recall correctly, promised annual grants of Rp. 1 billion to every village in Indonesia. If only one-quarter of this sum was set aside each year for the purchase of farmland, villages could build up their stock of collective property quite rapidly.

The principle of converting 'neglected' farm, plantation or forest lands into 'village social land banks' and allocating plots of this land to those who need it most (poor households, women heads of households, etc.) is in line with existing laws and apparently already being practiced in parts of Central Java.[41]

5.3. WHERE PRIVATE PROPERTY IN LAND EXISTS, PUTTING A CAP ON ACCUMULATION AND SPECULATION

This can be done by national and regional land reform laws (establishing maximum permitted holding sizes, and prohibiting absentee ownership, as in Indonesia's Basic Agrarian Law of 1960) but can also be organized locally.

In one of the sample villages in Central Java studied in Akatiga's recent research on food self-sufficiency in rice-growing regions, a prosperous villager made several land purchases until he had a total of 4.5 ha of irrigated rice land. Although this is still below the upper limit of 5.0 ha specified in the Basic Agrarian Law, a decision of the village government made it impossible for villagers who wanted to sell land, to sell it to this person. The village community had decided, simply, that this was enough and they did not want to live in a community marked by gross inequalities in land.

In short, there is no reason why communities should not democratically determine their own land ceilings, and adjust them periodically to adapt to changing situations.

[41] 'Kemandirian beras sebagai bagian kemandirian pangan', unpublished note, Bandung, Akatiga, October 2014.

5.3.1. *Promoting collectively-owned commercial farming, for export and domestic markets*

'Large versus small' in fact may not be the most crucial point in envisaging farming futures. It is at least possible to imagine a large-*size* farm production unit which is based on the characteristic features of small-*scale* farming:[42] low-input and mixed cropping rather than high-input monocrop cultivation, using artisanal and employment-enhancing rather than capital-intensive and labour-shedding techniques, which is water-saving, earth-cooling and sustainable and maintains the dignity, food security and labour incomes of those who work in it, which supports a vibrant and engaged local community, and which is based on principles of agrarian and environmental justice rather than corporate profit maximization. Only it is rather hard to imagine that socially responsible large farm units of this type would be based on corporate capital rather than collective or cooperative ownership.

Despite the apparent (and tragic) collapse of the farmer cooperative vision in Indonesia (largely due to excessive government interference and the emergence of predators among local elites and cooperative officials) there are isolated cases of successful, collectively-owned agri-export businesses. One interesting example of this is the Wangunwatie rubber plantation in Tasikmalaya, West Java. By an accident of history this formerly European-owned plantation became a cooperative in 1952 and is still collectively owned and managed by its members. They export Class A rubber sheets to Singapore, pay their workers (who are also cooperative members) more than the minimum wage, they have a well-working Askes health-insurance programme, build schools and other infrastructure for the community, and offer advisory services to local rubber farmers outside the cooperative. Members also have their own individual smallholder plots for food and market production, which were distributed equally to members in an autonomous (pre-BAL) land reform process. Paradoxically, the issuance of formal land titles on these plots by BPN some years ago – that is, the conversion of use rights to ownership rights – has led to the expected chronic process of differentiation so that control of these plots is now quite unequal.[43]

---

42 For the distinction between 'size' and 'scale' see J.-D. van der Ploeg, *The Art of Peasant Farming*, Halifax, Fernwood Publishing 2013.

43 D. Novrian, *Menempatkan kembali koperasi petani sebagai gerakan tani: Studi kasus Koperasi Petani Ciwangun*. Jakarta, University of Indonesia, MA thesis 2013.

5.3.2. *Providing and protecting equal land rights for women*

Land laws and land reforms are not democratic 'unless women achieve rights, autonomy, and better life chances within them', and there is no reason why men's and women's land rights should not be exactly the same.[44] Among Southeast Asian countries I believe it is the Philippines which has made most progress in this area. If I understand correctly, all new land certificates issued to someone who is married (male or female) bear the names of both partners, and the consent and signatures of both partners are required for any transaction involving that land.

5.3.3. *Promoting access to land for young farmers*

The FAO's recent report on *Youth and agriculture* includes case studies from the Philippines, Burkina Faso, Ethiopia, Mexico, Egypt and Uganda which all highlight possible means of improving youth's access to land. In Burkina Faso, the 8,000 member organization Songtaab-Yelgre negotiates with village chiefs and elders to provide women with access to land for shea butter production and has managed in this way to acquire land rights for 800 young women. In the northern Tigray region of Ethiopia, the NGO REST works on rehabilitation of barren hillside lands with soil and water conservation infrastructure so that these lands can be allocated to landless youth. The youth that benefit from the project are organized in associations which formulate their own land management by-laws to prevent misuse of these land grants. In some of the poorest regions of Mexico the Government has initiated the 'Rural entrepreneur and land fund programme', which assists young people to acquire underutilized former common lands, and also incentives to older landholders to transfer their land to the younger generation by providing social welfare schemes for their retirement. The Egyptian Government has a programme to make reclaimed desert land available to young graduates. Several thousand young people have obtained farms in this way. They are not allowed to sell their farms, and many of them have become successful producers of commercial vegetables for agribusiness, the tourist centres and for export. The Taiwan Council of Agriculture (COA) launched the 'Small Landlords, Large Tenants Programme' in 2008. The main purpose of this programme is to encourage elderly farmers to lease their land on a long-term basis to young farmers and to farmers' organizations. Within two years the programme had matched more than 8,000 elderly landowners with about 700 young-generation tenants, who now have on average 8 ha of land each, about seven times the national average farm size. In South-West Uganda, the agro-trading company RUL enters into short-term lease agreements with elderly landowners that do not wish or do not have the capacity to utilize their land in

---

[44] Jacobs, *Gender and Land Reform*, p. 192.

the foreseeable 12 months. Once RUL and the landowner agree on the terms of the lease between RUL and the owner and on the method of payment (cash or a proportion of the produce), and once the Uganda Land Commission approves the lease, RUL communicates the availability of the land to current or prospective youth groups through noticeboards in the community and the RUL extension workers. Youth groups should at least have eight members (aged 18–35), three of which must be female, in order to be able to apply for the lease.[45]

We could continue multiplying these concrete examples but I hope the general point is already clear. For each of the seven criteria which I mentioned, concrete and creative ways to fulfil them exist in one or another corner of the world, and in many corners of Indonesia. It would be useful to find better ways to communicate these possibilities to agrarian movements, agrarian researchers, law-makers and policy-makers, who often seem not to be aware of them.

[45] Food and Agriculture Organization, *Youth and Agriculture* (note 39).

NOTE ON CONTRIBUTORS

Prof. **Fons Coomans** holds the UNESCO Chair in Human Rights and Peace at the Department of International and European Law at Maastricht University. He teaches international human rights law and international development law at the School of Law. He is the Director of the Maastricht Centre for Human Rights, and Senior Researcher at the Netherlands School of Human Rights Research. His fields of research include the international protection of economic, social and cultural rights in a globalized society and the right to education, health and food in particular, as well as international monitoring mechanisms in the field of human rights and the extraterritorial application of human rights law. He is a Visiting Professor at the University of Cape Town. He has also collaborated with FIAN, a leading human rights NGO working on right to food issues.

Prof. Dr. **Michael G. Faure** LL.M. became academic director of the Maastricht European institute for transnational legal research (METRO) and professor of Comparative and International Environmental Law at the law faculty of Maastricht University in September 1991. He still holds both positions today.

In addition, he is academic director of the Ius Commune Research School and member of the board of directors of Ectil. Since the first of February 2008, he is half time professor of comparative private law and economics at the Rotterdam Institute of Law & Economics (RILE) of the Erasmus University in Rotterdam and academic director of the European Doctorate in Law and Economics (EDLE) programme.

Since 1982 he is equally attorney at the Antwerp Bar.

He publishes in the areas of environmental (criminal) law, tort and insurance and economic analysis of (accident) law.

Roman Herre has an M.A. in Geography (minoring in ethnology) from Westfälische Wilhelms-Universität Münster. Since 2007 he is a senior policy adviser for land, agriculture and rural development of the German section of the international human rights organization FIAN. His main activities include in-depth case work on selected cases of land conflicts with an actual focus on cases in Cambodia and Zambia, human rights expertise on land conflicts, agrarian reform and related policy analysis (e.g. land, agrofuel and trade policy). He has published multiple papers, including in peer review academic journals. He is also part of national and international networking, academic research in rural land related conflicts and consultation of governments and NGOs.

Elin Hilwig (LL.M.) has worked in the fields of human rights law and gender equality with various organizations. Among other things, in 2006 she headed an investigation into the functioning of a micro-financing project for the empowerment of women for developmental aid organisation Bless, in India. In 2007, she investigated human rights violations in the West Bank for human rights organisation Al Haq, in Ramallah. Most recently, between 2013–2014, she conducted a study on the feasibility of land-rights programming in conflict-affected Northern Uganda for developmental aid organisation War Child Canada, in Uganda. Additionally, she has spent a significant part of her career (2006–2013 & 2014–2015) working as a lawyer with a focus on immigration- and criminal defence cases in the Netherlands. Currently, Elin is a policy officer in the Sub-Sahara Africa Department of the Netherlands Ministry of Foreign Affairs in The Hague. She contributed to this publication in her personal capacity.

Dr. **Ingrid Westendorp** is a senior lecturer and researcher in International Law and Woman and Law with the International and European Law Department of Maastricht University. She conducts research on economic and social human rights, particularly the rights to housing and land, and issues concerning human rights of women such as domestic violence and gender equality in the context of culture. Furthermore, she is interested in doing research in Indonesia, especially the development of the rule of law concerning land rights for women. She teaches bachelor courses in International Law at the Faculty of Law and at the University College Maastricht, and a master course on Human Rights of Women in the context of the master's programme Globalisation and Law of the Faculty of Law. She coordinates a NUFFIC subsidized 4-year project on capacity building International Law at the Faculty of Law of the Padjadaran University in Bandung, Indonesia and she participates in the research project 'Mail Order Brides' of the European Parliament.

Dr. **Andri Wibisana** graduated from the Faculty of Law, Universitas Indonesia in 1998, from the Master Programme on Law and Economics, Utrecht University, the Netherlands in 2002, and from the Doctoral Programmme of the Faculty of Law, Maastricht University also in the Netherlands in 2008. His research interests cover environmental law, risk regulation, climate change law, and the economic analysis of law.

He joined the Faculty of Law, University of Indonesia in Jakarta in 1998. He teaches international environmental law (to undergraduate and master students), economic analysis of law (to undergraduate students), environmental law (to master students), and writing skills (to doctoral students).

From 2008–2010 he conducted post-doctoral research funded by the Royal Netherlands Academy of Arts and Sciences. In 2013 he was granted a scholarship from the Fulbright Senior Research Programme. For this purpose, he conducted research on REDD and climate change law at the Center for Climate Change Law, Columbia Law School from October 2013 until April 2014.

Prof. **Ben White** is an emeritus professor of sociology of the Institute of Social Studies (ISS) Erasmus University in The Hague. His area of expertise comprises agricultural sociology in particular in Indonesia. He has conducted several studies on Indonesia, where in total he lived for ten years in Yogyakarta and in Bogor. He works on agrarian change and the anthropology and history of childhood and youth, mainly in Indonesia. He is the (co)author of numerous books and publications. At ISS he teaches the course Political Economy/Ecology of Agriculture and Environment.

MAASTRICHT SERIES IN HUMAN RIGHTS

The *Maastricht Centre for Human Rights* facilitates and supports research in the field of human rights at Maastricht University's Faculty of Law. Research conducted at the Centre is interdisciplinary, with a focus on public international law, criminal law and social sciences. Titles appearing in the Maastricht Series in Human Rights have been peer reviewed under the responsibility of the Board of the Centre.

Published titles within the Series:

1. Ineke Boerefijn, Fons Coomans, Jenny Goldschmidt, Rikki Holtmaat and Ria Wolleswinkel (eds.), *Temporary Special Measures. Accelerating de facto Equality of Women under Article 4(1) UN Convention on the Elimination of All Forms of Discrimination against Women* (2003)
   ISBN 90-5095-359-X
2. Fons Coomans and Menno T. Kamminga (eds.), *Extraterritorial Application of Human Rights Treaties* (2004)
   ISBN 90-5095-394-8
3. Koen De Feyter and Felipe Gómez Isa (eds.), *Privatisation and Human Rights in the Age of Globalisation* (2005)
   ISBN 90-5095-422-7
4. Ingrid Westendorp and Ria Wolleswinkel (eds.), *Violence in the domestic sphere* (2005)
   ISBN 90-5095-526-6
5. Fons Coomans (ed.), *Justiciability of Economic and Social Rights* (2006)
   ISBN 978-90-5095-582-9
6. Jan C.M. Willems (ed.), *Developmental and Autonomy Rights of Children: Empowering Children, Caregivers and Communities. 2nd revised edition* (2007)
   ISBN 978-90-5095-726-7
7. Alette Smeulers and Roelof Haveman (eds.), *Supranational Criminology: Towards a Criminology of International Crimes* (2008)
   ISBN 978-90-5095-791-5
8. Hans van Crombrugge, Wouter Vandenhole and Jan C.M. Willems (eds.), *Shared Pedagogical Responsibility* (2008)
   ISBN 978-90-5095-813-4

9. Hildegard Schneider and Peter Van den Bossche (eds.), *Protection of Cultural Diversity from a European and International Perspective* (2008)
ISBN 978-90-5095-864-6
10. Fons Coomans, Fred Grünfeld and Menno T. Kamminga (eds.), *Methods of Human Rights Research* (2009)
ISBN 978-90-5095-879-0
11. Jan C.M. Willems (ed.), *Children's Rights and Human Development. A Multidisciplinary Reader* (2010)
ISBN 978-94-000-0032-2
12. Martine Boersma and Hans Nelen (eds.), *Corruption & Human Rights: Interdisciplinary Perspectives* (2010)
ISBN 978-94-000-0085-8
13. Hans Nelen and Jacques Claessen (eds.), *Beyond the Death Penalty* (2012)
ISBN 978-1-78068-060-6
14. Fons Coomans and Rolf Künneman (eds.), *Cases and Concepts on Extraterritorial Obligations in the Area of Economic, Social and Cultural Rights* (2012)
ISBN 978-94-000-0046-9
15. Chen Weidong and Taru Spronken (eds.), *Three Approaches to Combating Torture in China* (2012)
ISBN 978-1-78068-088-0
16. Michele Panzavolta, Dorris de Vocht, Marc Van Oosterhout and Miet Vanderhallen (eds.), *Interrogating Young Suspects. Procedural Safeguards from a Legal Perspective* (2015)
ISBN 978-1-78068-299-0
17. Miet Vanderhallen, Marc van Oosterhout, Michele Panzavolta and Dorris de Vocht (eds.), *Interrogating Young Suspects. Procedural Safeguards from an Empirical Perspective* (2016)
ISBN 978-1-78068-301-0
18. Roland Moerland, Hans Nelen and Jan Willems (eds.), *Denialism and Human Rights* (2016)
ISBN 978-1-78068-369-0

www.ingramcontent.com/pod-product-compliance
Ingram Content Group UK Ltd.
Pitfield, Milton Keynes, MK11 3LW, UK
UKHW051928100926
8556IPUK00022B/1428

9 781780 684413